SOLO
DIVING

THE ART OF UNDERWATER SELF-SUFFICIENCY

ROBERT VON MAIER

Solo Diving

The Art of Underwater Self-Sufficiency

by Robert von Maier

Mark F. Nelson
4 Harriet St.
Centereach, N.Y. 11720

Watersport Publishing, Inc.
Post Office Box 83727
San Diego, CA 92138

Cover photo by Al Bruton

First Printing 1991
Watersport Publishing, Inc., P.O. Box 83727, San Diego, CA 92138

Printed in the United States

**International Standard Book Number
ISBN 0-922769-13-3**

Library of Congress Catalog Card Number: 91-65028
von Maier, Robert
      Solo Diving
      The Art of Underwater Self-Sufficiency

To Jillie

Critic, Confidante, and Loving Companion

Table of Contents

Acknowledgements

This book would not have been possible without the assistance of a great many individuals. First of all, I'd like to thank my publisher, Ken Loyst, and all the good people at Watersport Publishing, Inc. (especially Denise Winslett, who's gradually coaching me into computer literacy). Christopher Pyle (say hello to Ish and Pepe for me), Lance Milbrand (Hollywood awaits!), Darren Webb (a.k.a. Commander Deep), Tab Brewer (power one for me), Heather McSharry (student extraordinaire), Ranee Rosser (more illustrations next book) - thanks for all the assistance and support. A special word of thanks to Dr. Lee Somers, Al Bruton, Michael Menduno, and Brett Gilliam for their timely contributions. To all the individuals whose opinions appear in Chapter 6, thank you for your enlightened responses - they add a very important dimension to this text. Also, many thanks to all the various manufacturers who rendered their time, efforts, and materials so that this work could be completed. And again, for all her love and support (not to mention the editing), a sincere word of appreciation for Jill Burch.

Robert von Maier
San Diego, California

Foreword

So, how safe is the buddy system? With the information now available, it is still impossible to determine the statistical significance of the buddy system in the prevention of diving fatalities. However, when the figures for sport diving fatalities are compared to the total number of divers (and dives), it can be said that both the U.S. Navy and the recreational diving communities have excellent safety records. And it must be acknowledged that the buddy system has been the cornerstone of diving safety since the beginning of modern scuba diving. It is possible that the weakness is not in the buddy system, but in the buddies! It is very likely that a general improvement in buddy diving techniques and attitudes could prevent many diving accidents.

How can you be sure your diving buddy will be able to help you if you get in trouble? How can you be sure that you are a good diving buddy as well? To help answer these questions, I prepared an earlier paper on the fundamental rules for buddy diving, the qualities of a good diver, criteria for selecting a good buddy, undesirable diver personalities, and why some divers prefer to dive solo.

Although the buddy system is considered by many to be the cornerstone of scuba diving safety, I can't dismiss the fact that divers continue to die even though the buddy system is being used. Is it because of the inability of the buddy to assist in an emergency? Is it simply a "lip service" acceptance of the buddy system and a disregard for it in practice? Subjective observation of a number of divers in the field suggested that they truly attempted to adhere to the principles of the buddy system. Yet, once these divers were underwater were they real buddies or just two independent divers in the same ocean that happen to be relatively close to each other?

In talking to many "old timers" I hear tales of horror relating the incidences where they almost lost their lives as the result of the actions of a buddy. Some of these individuals simply refuse to rely on or be responsible for another individual underwater. Others, including many instructors, simply want to be free of responsibility every so often. So, they simply slip below the waves for a few moments of peace and solitude. They love diving and they love the ocean. They just want to be alone in this underwater environment once in awhile. How often have you taken a quiet walk alone in the woods or a park simply to be alone with yourself and your thoughts?

Other divers seek adventure. Like other adventurers, they find that the solo experience sometimes adds dimension to their quest for adventure. Mount Everest has been conquered by a solo climber. Subjectively, I feel that there are an increasing number of closet solo divers.

One former instructor and very experienced diver indicated that the only time he had ever come close to death in diving was at the hands of a panicked buddy. In reflection, I realize that my only personal close calls in 30 years of recreational diving have been as a result of a buddy or in diving with a group of previously unknown divers. The results have included decompression sickness, abandonment in a Florida cave, and forced independent emergency ascents.

Recently, I faced this realization with new meaning when I spent a week diving with a group of divers of unknown quality and capability. Physical condition ranged from excellent to frighteningly poor. One obese, out-of-shape beginning diver expounded on the concept that 100 foot ocean dives were a "piece of cake!" In my opinion, this individual should not have been in the ocean with scuba. Many of the group consumed large quantities of alcohol each day, some to excess. This is quite common among many vacationing divers today. But, the most obvious deviation from the standards of the recreational diving community was the fact that no one in the group had an alternate air source.

I was in the ocean with some very wonderful people. However, they were "unknowns" as far as their diving skill was concerned. They were apparently trained "buddy breathers," not alternate air source breathers. I have seen buddy breathing work. In fact, on this particular trip, a husband/wife team successfully dealt with an out-of-air situation by buddy breathing. They had been trained together. But, more often than not, I have observed buddy breathing failures in real emergencies. As a stranger to the group, could I rely on one of these divers to supply me with air in an emergency?

Based on observations during the first day of diving, I elected to dive solo. I did not want to accept the potential risk of an emergency situation with a diver of unknown capabilities. My decision was reinforced over the week by their drinking, "piece of cake" attitudes, and various other practices. Now, let me define what SOLO meant in this case. Even though I was diving in a group of 3 to 8 or more individuals, including a very capable dive guide, I simply did not elect to have a specific buddy. There were several reasons for this.

First, if I had an air supply failure, I would not have gone to one of the individual divers in the group to share air. Since none of them had alternate air sources, I did not want one of them to accept the responsibility of sharing air at depths up to 100 feet with a person they had never been in the water with before. I decided that I would either swim to the guide (who had an alternate air source) or make an emergency swimming ascent.

Second, I am a photographer. It is practically impossible to find a diving buddy among a group of strangers who is willing to devote their dive to staying beside a photographer who is taking 10 minutes to shoot a picture of an animal that means little or nothing to them. I didn't even wish to try.

Third, by swimming among the group rather than attempting to stay with a specific individual, I could observe the divers and have an alternate air source available if needed. My air consumption was among the lowest in the group and I made a point of reducing my attention to photography near the end of a dive and be in a position to provide air if needed.

As I reflected on my decision and reasons for that decision, I came to the realization that I generally consider myself to be a solo diver much of the time, even though I may be diving with a buddy. I am solo diving in the sense that I am always prepared to resolve any emergency that I might encounter - independent of the other diver(s).

Most instructors are, in a sense, solo diving every time they are in the water with students. They must be prepared to handle student emergencies and they must also be prepared to independently deal with any personal emergencies.

I hope that it is obvious to the readers of **SOLO DIVING: The Art of Underwater Self-Sufficiency** that I am not advocating that divers discard the traditional buddy system. Furthermore, I am not condoning dives where an individual, simply because they are a certified diver, goes to the ocean, far removed from the presence of others, and swims off into the blue. However, I can certainly respect the motivations of self-sufficient solo divers.

Will the time come in recreational diving where there is public pressure for a solo scuba diver certification? Maybe! Maybe not! In spite of the fundamental rule of buddy diving, there are an increasing number of divers who are currently practicing solo diving and it is for them that this book has been written.

Lee H. Somers, Ph.D.
The University of Michigan,
Department of Atmospheric,
Oceanic and Space Sciences

Introduction

One thing we cannot escape – forever afterward, throughout all our life, the memory of the magic of water and its life, of the home which was once our own – this will never leave us.

William Beebe

We live in a world where ideas and opinions are often deep-rooted and frequently outdated. Accepting those ideas and opinions is perhaps the easiest road to follow. Rejecting them takes one down a rather arduous and often ill-paved pathway.

As a diving instructor and a teacher by nature, I not only pursue increased knowledge and education for myself, but for my students as well. When a particular viewpoint has become obsolete or is in need of revision, I see no need to refrain from its correction. With the subject at hand – solo diving – I believe that the time for re-evaluation has indeed arrived.

Solo diving is and always will be an activity that involves risk. But then again, so is driving an automobile; and who among you has not done it solo? The fact that there are inherent risks in diving does not, or should not, imply that doing it alone is somehow wrong or perilous. In fact, to buddy-up two less-than-competent (i.e. buddy-dependent) divers is an unmistakable formula for disaster – quite the opposite of the intended purpose.

Periodically, the sport diving industry weighs the issue of solo diving in an effort to decide whether or not to sanction it. In the May/June 1989 issue of **Sources** magazine, Spence Campbell, a professional diving instructor and past General Manager of the Ocean Corporation responded quite aptly to the subject.

It makes no more sense to me that an individual cannot go diving by himself (or is at any more risk) than it would be to state that the same individual could not drive a car or fly an airplane alone. The FAA allows pilots to solo aircraft, which fly above homes and schoolhouses. These individuals could do tremendous damage, not just to themselves but to many others. Why is this considered less risky than diving alone?

Judging from the facts, a re-evaluation of both the buddy system and solo diving is undeniably in order. Perhaps this text will shed a bit of much needed light on an old and often controversial subject - solo diving.

About This Book

Being alone with the sea is definitive meditation. It is an awe-inspiring realm where the Gods must surely dwell – and yet – they too would require no companion, for the sea is companion enough.

John David Roberts

SOLO DIVING: The Art of Underwater Self-Sufficiency is intended for a general diving audience and not exclusively for advanced divers. However, common sense dictates that not all divers, simply by virtue of possessing a certification card, are either physically or mentally self-sufficient. Undoubtedly, there will always be a few who will never be self-sufficient for one reason or another (skill, training, self-confidence), and it is for these individuals that I strongly recommend further training and education with a qualified instructor, if for no other reason than to increase their knowledge and heighten the level of safety both for themselves and their buddies.

The material disclosed within these pages is the product of hundreds of hours of research both in and out of the water. It is not intended to be used as a self-study guide to solo diving. It is a written companion designed to complement and accompany proper training, experience, and perhaps most importantly, unreserved self-evaluation. Within it's seven chapters lies a plethora of information, much of it presented for the first time. The time spent researching, interviewing, writing, and processing this information has truly been an education in itself, an education in not only how the diving industry functions, but how people in general are willing to trade common sense and reality for politics and corporate dogma.

Photo by Ken Loyst

When I first ventured into the literary jungle in search of a publisher I was forewarned by my colleagues that a book about solo diving would undoubtedly be rejected. Something about going out on a limb... Well, in my blissful ignorance I ignored their chidings and continued in hot pursuit. At first, when I presented to Ken Loyst and Watersport Publishing, Inc. the idea for the work you have in front of you, the response was anything but negative. The initial concern was not about the controversial subject material (Ken has always been a rebel), but rather about the timeframe in which I could have the book completed. It appeared that my colleagues were mistaken, this wouldn't be so difficult after all.

Sure people solo dive, but getting them to openly discuss it (especially when the discussion may end up in published form) is another thing entirely. It seemed as if no one wanted to come out of the proverbial closet and actually confront reality. They would, however, offer their opinions in cautious, guarded form. The prospects looked bleak; a book to write with damn few materials to reference and no one to consult. It wasn't until I confronted many of the individuals whose opinions you'll find in Chapter 6 that I began to realize I'd been talking to the wrong people. Often, the most verbal critics of a particular activity are in fact the ones who clandestinely practice it. (Funny, but a couple of TV evangelists come to mind right about now.) You see, solo diving is more common than many would like to admit, and it's not, as they would have you believe, a dangerous and reckless form of diving. It is, however, an activity that shouldn't be conducted by just anyone. It requires, as I've explained throughout these pages, 110% competency and proficiency as well as a strong working knowledge of the particular area to be dived.

I've included in each chapter information that is specifically intended for solo divers. However, those of you who don't wish to go solo (and I have many friends who fit into this category who are competent, self-sufficient divers) will find the material to be useful just the same. I have blended new information with old to create a source of reference that, to the best of my knowledge, is the first volume of its kind to be published expressly with the solo diver in mind. Also, I have included the section *Reference Materials* so that one may have access to further information over and above what has been included here. Finally, a glossary of over 150 diving and diving-related terms from areas such as physiology, medicine, marine biology, and oceanography appears in the back of the book.

Solo diving is not for everyone. But for those who wish to make the experience a safe and enjoyable one, I sincerely hope that this volume will serve as an educated reference.

Chapter 1

The Buddy System

Fear is the motivation for the buddy system. Divers don't want to drown and they don't want to be eaten. There's nothing strange in this fear; what's strange is the response to it: get a buddy.

Bob Halstead

I'm not saying that every diver immediately drops their buddy and goes diving alone, however, it's time that all instructional agencies stop giving divers the false sense of security that their buddy will be there to save them.

**Glen Fitzler,
Co-Owner, Truth Aquatics**

Genesis

As a child, I remember being told that there's safety in numbers. If you were sent to the school principal's office for some type of mischievous behavior (not me of course, I was an angel), it was somehow consoling to have one of your classmates as a partner in crime. At least that way you didn't have to go it alone.

Eventually, I found myself involved in a most fascinating sport – scuba diving. The old axiom "safety in numbers" was there once again. This time they referred to it as the buddy system; a concept that apparently has its roots in the old YMCA maxim which maintains that one should never swim alone. Another explanation for its implementation stems from military diving. At one time, all military diving was conducted with at least some type of surface support mechanism such as that utilized with the old Navy Mark V rigs. When scuba became a viable option, tethered or umbilical diving wasn't always necessary, therefore in order to keep track of the working diver a "buddy" was implemented. I have interviewed several retired Navy divers from the United States and Great Britain who were actively involved in many aspects of military diving. They informed me that at no time during their training were they taught to rely on a buddy for their own safety. On the other hand, I was initially taught that my buddy was not only necessary for my safety, but if I even thought of entering the water solo all hell would break loose. How could I possibly deal with an emergency if I didn't have a buddy?

Well, this fallacy soon toppled as I began to dive by myself with increasing regularity. Dive after dive, year after year and not once

Illustration by Ranee Rosser

20

did I find myself in a situation where a buddy was required – not once. I still occasionally made dives with a buddy, but I did so only if I knew that they were competent, self-sufficient divers like myself that didn't need to rely on me for their own safety.

Where's My Buddy?

Too often I see divers at the beach who are "buddy hunting." They have been trained to adhere to the buddy system without exception, even if it means buddying-up with a complete stranger - as long as they have a buddy.

It doesn't take a rocket scientist to see the inadequacies in this type of reasoning. Any buddy is not better than no buddy. In fact, in many (perhaps most) cases the buddy system fails miserably in the single, most important area that it was designed for – safety.

Does the buddy system really make diving any safer?

Photo by Darren Webb

The misconception that buddy diving is safer than solo diving is definitely not substantiated by reality. Let's consider the facts: for most divers, the concept of the buddy system translates into same day, same ocean (not exactly what they were taught in their Open Water/Entry Level course). Nevertheless, the majority of divers tend to separate, for one reason or another, during the course of their dive. Either they did not share the same interest (sight-seeing, photography, hunting, etc.) or they were incompatible due to various other reasons such as skill level, physical conditioning, or, in some cases, temperament.

I have seen divers who claim to be a buddy team on the surface, but in reality, conveniently lose each other as soon as they enter the water. In other instances, I have watched as one diver waits patiently (or not so patiently) while another, his/her buddy, swims up and down in the water column, attempting to clear their ears.

In many situations I have overheard two buddies discussing the fact that they spent their entire dive trying to locate one another. Or worse yet, while one buddy was in distress, the other failed to recognize the problem, thus forsaking his/her primary role as a buddy.

Does the buddy system really make diving any safer? Of course not, particularly as it is so often taught and practiced by the diving community. Definitively, the buddy system is a practice wherein two or more divers with equal experience and skill levels, sharing the same interests, continually monitor each other (including gauges) before, during, and after the dive, constantly remaining within close proximity to one another should immediate assistance be necessary.

This is a nice, neat little scenario that looks great in theory, but rarely comes to pass. The only time that detailed buddy skills are usually practiced is during some form of open water training in a supervised environment. I am not advocating the dissolution of the buddy system. In fact, my intent is quite the opposite. I merely wish to bring out of the closet, once and for all, the hard reality that solo diving – if practiced safely and prudently – is not foolish or ill-advised. It is merely another type of sport diving that is safely performed by divers all over the world in myriad environments.

Weighing The Options

There are obviously situations where the presence of a skillful, competent, self-sufficient buddy would be prudent, and yes, may even add a degree of safety. The key words are skillful, competent and self-sufficient. A diver, any diver, who does not possess the necessary skills and confidence to be self-sufficient in at least some underwater environments is desperately in need of additional training and education.

I would not expect a newly certified diver to descend onto the *Andrea Doria* alone and feel confidently self-sufficient, although there are highly experienced wreck/deep divers who do just this. In fact, one very knowledgeable and experienced wreck/deep diver that

I spoke with made a very valid point; he stated that on dives such as these where the depth and nature of the dive prohibits all but the most advanced divers (in this situation, a very select few), it is not only difficult to find a buddy with the proper skills and knowledge, but due to the nature and profile of the activity, it is perhaps more prudent to go solo. In other types of diving such as kelp and cave diving I would not only expect a diver new to these scenarios to desire a more knowledgeable buddy, but to also seek proper training and instruction before attempting them. These are situations that are all too obvious. However, they present some interesting questions: When is it not prudent to dive alone, and why?

Sport diving can be grouped into three basic, fundamental categories based on the degree of risk involved, as well as the level of skill and/or special training necessary to safely accomplish the dive. The three categories are as follows:

Low-Risk

This type of dive would involve an environment that is relatively free of natural hazards such as sharp rocks or out-croppings, unpredictable water conditions (tides, currents, surf, surge, etc.) or hazardous marine life. It would be in a location that could safely be dived from

A low-risk environment is relatively free of natural hazards such as sharp rocks or out-croppings, unpredictable water conditions or hazardous marine life.

Photo by Ken Loyst

the shore and would not require a long, arduous surface swim or a boat. Also, it would ideally be an area that is regularly patrolled by lifeguards or the equivalent. Depth of a dive in this category would generally not exceed 40 feet (12m).

Moderate-Risk

The possibilities here are nearly limitless, but would include such factors as rocks, reefs, kelp, moderate surge, moderate surf, various types of marine life, shallow-water wrecks, and may require a lengthy surface swim or boat. The location would be somewhat more remote than a low-risk dive site. Depth of a dive at a moderate-risk dive site would generally not exceed 60 feet (18m).

A moderate-risk environment would include such factors as rocks, reefs, kelp, moderate surge, etc.

Due to the additional risk-creating factors of this category, one can clearly see that a greater degree of self-sufficiency, skill, and experience would be in order to safely dive in such an area.

High-Risk

Again, the list of limiting factors is very extensive, and would include, but not be limited to, elements such as caves, steep submarine canyons, deep water reefs or wrecks as well as shallow water wrecks that are of an unsafe, precarious nature (e.g. unsealed hatches or entryways, cables, explosives, a deteriorated or unstable constitution, etc.).

Additionally, a dive considered high-risk could entail intentional interaction with potentially dangerous animals. Other obvious factors are heavy, high-energy surf, heavy surge, strong, unpredictable currents, ice diving (including diving in water that is extremely cold, although the perception of what constitutes cold water is somewhat individualistic), high-elevation diving, remote location, and a plethora of additional, more localized hazards.

Any dive that exceeds 60 feet (18m) would be considered by some as a high-risk dive. However, this again is a situation where degree of self-sufficiency, skill, and experience comes into play.

This photo of a research diver conducting a deep dive at Scripps Canyon, San Diego, California, is a prime example of a high-risk environment.

Photo by Darren Webb

The above-listed categories are to be used as references only and are not to be considered concrete examples of either low-, moderate-, or high-risk diving. Obviously, depending upon the training and skill level of the diver in question, the distinction from one category to the next will vary greatly. Common sense is the all-important watchword.

Considering these categories, one can see that a dive made in a low-risk location would not necessarily require a buddy. However, as we move into the moderate-risk category, whether or not a buddy is necessary is dependent upon the diver involved as well as his/her familiarity with the particular dive site. (Keep in mind the fact that no buddy team should consist of divers that are buddy-dependent, no matter what the risk factors involved. The term "necessary" as used above is meant in a general sense only and not to be construed as meaning necessary for safety. The only "necessary" buddy would be an instructor in a training situation.) On the other hand, any diving that is conducted in a high-risk environment would wisely take into account the benefits of a skillful, competent, self-sufficient buddy. There are, as I mentioned above, definite exceptions.

I wish to point out that when referring to a buddy I qualify the term by including the adjectives skillful, competent, and self-sufficient. As stated earlier in the chapter, a dive made with a buddy who is poorly trained or dependent upon another diver is better attempted alone or not at all, particularly when the issue of safety is considered. Furthermore, if a buddy is opted for, make sure that the individual doesn't present more of a liability than a benefit.

The concept of the buddy system is most definitely not outdated, although it is certainly in need of serious reorganization. With the advent of today's high-tech dive gear and a body of ever-increasing knowledge about a once little-known subject – scuba diving – the controversial, shrouded world of solo diving can finally be elevated to an art.

In Chapter 2 we will briefly examine the development of sport diver training. We will also investigate the concepts of self-evaluation and self-regulation and why their initiation is critical to diving safety – particularly when diving solo.

Chapter 2

The Self-Sufficient Diver

One inescapable conclusion, however, is that buddy diving, as commonly practiced, does not offer ironclad protection from accidental drowning. No matter how you choose to dive, proper planning and training, combined with moment-to-moment attention and care, are the best insurance against mishap.

Dr. Tom Millington

Considering the unforgiving nature of mistakes in diving, just talking about advanced and high-tech diving has to be done with caution, lest it lead innocent lambs to the slaughter.

R.W. Bill Hamilton, Ph.D..

Evolution of Diver Training

Back in the days when scuba diving was first evolving into a sport, the types of people who initially braved the depths with mask, fins, and Aqualung were generally those who spent a great deal of time in and around the ocean. They were, for the most part, avid free divers who thought nothing of plunging down 50 or so feet on a single breath. (I'd like to see how many so-called "advanced divers" could do that today.) These were the true water people who pioneered our sport. They became, and gave rise to, the first scuba diving instructors.

Initially, diving instruction was quite basic. It had to be, not much was known about it. An open water class generally consisted of a brief equipment orientation (the equipment was typically military surplus or a garage-built facsimile), and a few key phrases - something about not holding your breath and surfacing below your smallest bubbles. The brave adventurer was then led to the water's edge and turned loose. If he (and it was most often "he") was lucky, his instructor even got into the water with him, but not always. (Remember, these were the days when wetsuits, even in moderately chilly water, were not always readily available, and as for BCD's...)

Things are done a bit more thoroughly these days, and for good reason. The average entry level student of today is considerably different than the average neophyte of yesteryear. Not only are today's students from wide and varied backgrounds, but age and level of fitness are also influencing factors that are more involved than they once were *(See Chapter 4)*.

Not only are today's students from wide and varied backgrounds, but age and level of fitness are also influencing factors that are more involved than they once were.

Photo by Ken Loyst

Not only is today's instruction more detailed, but the equipment is, in many ways, easier to use.

Photo by Darren Webb

The now outdated image of scuba diving being strictly for the macho types actually has a basis in fact. As eluded to above, the instruction as well as the equipment was rather limited and required an individual to be a bit hardier than most. Conversely, not only is today's instruction more detailed, but the equipment is, in many ways, easier to use. Thus, a potential diver need not be as stalwart as his/her predecessors. This brings us to an important question: With an ever-increasing population of sport divers, many of whom are not "water people", how many of them: A) Shouldn't be diving at all, and B) Need to better understand the concept of self-sufficiency?

Self-Evaluation

The road to underwater self-sufficiency is not the same for all divers. Some individuals, for one reason or another, are more inclined to be water people. For these divers, establishing skill and confidence in the water is almost second nature. For others, it requires a bit more effort to achieve the same level of watermanship (i.e. self-sufficiency). And then there are those who, no matter how much training and education they receive, will never become self-sufficient divers in any water environment. For the latter, I contend that they should either not be certified, or not dive without the direct supervision of an instructor.

In the process of researching this book, I made it a point to speak to dozens of diving instructors from many facets of the sport diving industry. In all cases, I would nonchalantly bring up the subject of solo diving and then sit back and mentally record their opinions and observations. Darren Webb, a good friend and colleague, offered one of the most interesting and thought-provoking viewpoints. He stated that out of all the certified divers he'd observed both in and out

Levels of self-sufficiency vary and not all divers are self-sufficient in the same areas.

of the water, most were in need of further training and education, not for the purpose of becoming self-sufficient, but merely to be fundamentally competent with the most basic skills. This is where self-evaluation comes into play.

For an individual to be completely self-sufficient underwater is certainly the most desirable end result in diver training. Realistically, not all divers are either capable of this (in a complete, definitive sense), or have a desire to achieve it. In fact, for many sport divers, solo diving just doesn't present the same appeal as it does for others. Perhaps they prefer a buddy for personal reasons such as companionship, or they simply feel more comfortable having someone along for the dive. These are reasons that, in this author's opinion, are valid and present no real problems. The problems arise when a buddy is desired to maintain an individual's safety (i.e. to compensate for poor watermanship or inadequate training).

An integral part of self-evaluation involves a thorough understanding of the concept of underwater self-sufficiency; a concept that is comprised of myriad phases or stages. As would be expected, one diver's level of self-sufficiency could be dramatically different from another's. For this reason, it is crucial for a diver to know his/her limitations, particularly when diving solo. (When diving with a buddy, it is equally important to know their limitations.)

If we refer back to Chapter 1 and review the three categories of sport diving (low-, moderate-, high-risk), the idea that underwater self-sufficiency has various stages makes good sense. Before a dive can safely be made, particularly a solo dive, the diver should first consider the following questions:

1) What risks are inherent in this dive, and would they be better met with a competent buddy who is experienced in this type of diving, or who's more familiar with this location?

2) If a qualified buddy is desired, am I self-sufficient enough so that I won't be a liability to him/her?

3) If I decide to dive solo, am I confident that my physical abilities, skills, training, and experience (all measures of self-sufficiency) such that I can safely make this dive?

4) Is there any special gear or equipment (lights, line, marker buoy, etc.) that is required?

5) Are there any additional considerations that need to be addressed to safely execute this dive?

Any dive can be attempted. However, whether or not it falls within the parameters that define safety is dependent upon how an individual answers the five questions above. Be advised that it is quite possible to add to the list, and it is up to the diver in question to take into account any further details that may be of consequence.

Self-Regulation

For self-evaluation to be successful a diver must be completely honest with him/herself and determine if and how the dive should be made. I've had divers tell me that they attempted a particular dive because of peer pressure (sound familiar?). They soon came to the realization that safety and common sense were exchanged for bravado. Another attitude that I've encountered involves a similar scenario. Debating whether they should make the dive or not (this in itself should answer the question), the diver takes the opinion that "Well, I won't know until I've tried it." Wrong answer-if you don't know, don't be foolish enough to attempt it.

Additionally, I've seen seasick, fatigued divers on boat charters who, because they paid for the trip, wanted to push themselves into another dive. When, as divemaster, I inform them that they're done diving for the day their usual response is "Whadda ya mean, I paid for three dives and I'm gonna make three dives!" Wrong again. *Mal de mer*, fatigue and a less-than-level head is a sure combination for disaster *(See Table 2.1 for tips on avoiding seasickness)*. Once again, common sense is a key factor in unreserved self-evaluation, a factor that all too often is discarded.

In addition to personal factors that may tell an individual to avoid a particular dive or type of diving, there may very well be other considerations that should be to be taken into account. The five questions referred to above address several issues that are predominantly concerned with individual proficiency or equipment considerations. There are, however, other elements that come into play that are just as important, and perhaps a bit more localized. An essential part of proper self-regulation involves decision making: Should I make this dive or would it be wise to abort? Even if all systems are go as far as the diver is concerned, what about Mother Nature?

Table 2.1

Tips on Avoiding Seasickness When Boat Diving

1) Avoid eating greasy foods or drinking caffeinated beverages prior to making a dive. Also, avoid sugary foods such as donuts and other pastries.

2) Be sure to take any seasickness medication well before the dive; it may even be wise to begin the medication the night before. Be advised that medication is not effective once the individual is seasick.

3) Seasickness medication should only be taken after consulting a physician. Transdermal medications that are usually applied via a patch behind the ear are not recommended when diving is involved.

4) Be sure to remain on deck to get plenty of fresh air and do not go below unless necessary.

5) Visual orientation is thought to be an important consideration in avoiding *Mal de mer*, therefore, whenever possible, it may be helpful to maintain eye contact with a stationary, land-based object or the horizon.

6) Avoid areas that are exposed to exhaust fumes (engine room, transom, etc.).

7) Avoid reading or writing while underway.

8) If you are prone to seasickness, be prepared to enter the water immediately upon arriving at the dive site. In many cases, mild nausea is eliminated by entering the water and making a dive. However, a diver experiencing anything more than mild nausea should remain onboard and rest in a cool, shaded area. It is also important to drink plenty of water to avoid dehydration.

9) Any degree of seasickness should be considered a contraindication to solo diving. Diving alone requires that the individual be without illness.

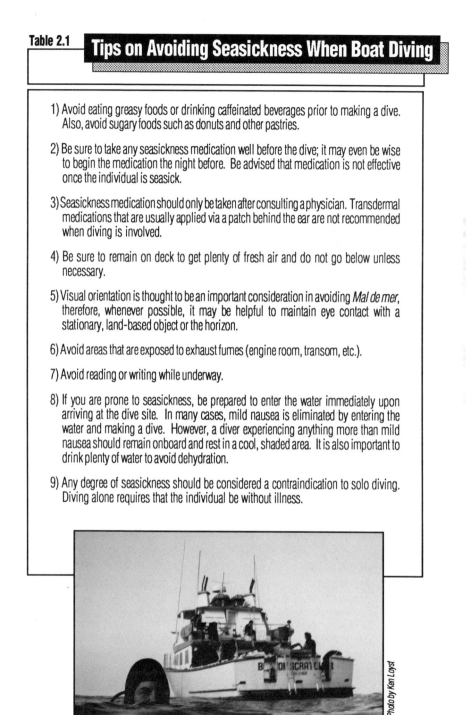

Photo by Ken Loyst

In all my years of diving, the single most influential factor responsible for scrapping myriad dives (ask any of my students) is Mother Nature. For divers, this translates into ocean conditions, above and below the water. Surf, surge, tides, and visibility are just a few examples. Depending on your particular geographic location, you may find it necessary to add to this list. If at all possible, water conditions should be checked prior to making all other preparations. This alone could save a great deal of unnecessary frustration and effort. After the conditions have been checked, mentally evaluate your skills and proficiency to determine if they are sufficient (in theory, they should be considerably more than sufficient) to deal with the prevailing conditions.

Photo by Darren Webb

Self-regulation means not getting in the water when conditions, all conditions, are less than optimal. The dual process of self-evaluation and self-regulation is not to be taken lightly. When conducted wisely and unreservedly, it is a plan of action that will assure a diver not only an enjoyable dive, but more importantly, a safe one that can be repeated.

In Chapter 3 we will discuss how physical as well as mental fitness affects a diver's performance and proficiency in the water. (If you consider yourself to be an "advanced diver" this is one chapter you won't want to miss.)

Chapter 3

Diving Fitness and Physiology

The human body is a great and noble machine. With proper care and routine maintenance its ability to perform is guaranteed. Neglect and apathy render it impotent and useless. How great a crime to dispose of such potentiality.
Thomas Michael Lehrbach

Vincit qui se vincit.
(First we must overcome our own bad habits.)
Anonymous

Measure For Measure

I personally have very little tolerance for apathy and laziness (except in koalas, of course). As Mr. Lehrbach stated so aptly, "The human body is a great and noble machine." I heartily and vociferously agree. If this is truly the case (as indeed it is), why don't more people treat it accordingly? I know what you're thinking: "Look von Maier, we don't need any more health gurus. Just shut up and hand me another beer." Well, health guru I'm not, and if it's another beer you want, perhaps you should make it something a bit stronger. You may need it for what's about to unfold.

My dictionary defines the term fit in a variety of ways. Below is an example of how it applies to this chapter.

fit (fit), adj., 1. adequately suited. 2. prepared or ready. 3. in good condition or health.

Now, using any of the three definitions above, I know of damn few sport divers who can honestly claim that they're 100% fit for diving (this includes instructors). As we saw in the proceeding chapters, training, education, experience, skill proficiency, and mental preparedness are all units of measure on the great yardstick (or, meterstick if you prefer) of underwater self-sufficiency. For those of you with an eye for the incredibly obvious, you've no doubt noticed by now that I've devoted an entire chapter, this chapter, to one additional unit of measure - physical fitness and preparedness.

As one might gather, and correctly so, physical fitness and preparedness is a most important ingredient in diver safety. All the training and education in the world cannot replace good physical conditioning. So perhaps it's time that you put down the light beer (I don't know about you, but the lighter the beer, the more of it I drank) and began swimming laps. Now, if you're another Rambo then perhaps you can afford to skip this chapter (you probably wouldn't be able to read it anyway). However, if you're like a large percentage of the sport divers that I've seen, your level of fitness is in dire need of improvement and the best time to start is now.

Whatever water environment you happen to be diving in, due to the fact that it is not our natural medium and at times can be very hostile, it stands to reason that the level of fitness necessary to maintain a degree of safety is higher than that required on land. (Obviously there are a few terrestrial activities that are exceptions to this rule.) Because of these physical considerations, a diver needs to maintain a minimal degree of fitness – particularly the solo diver.

Solo diving requires that a diver be capable of fending for him/ herself and not be buddy-dependent. If upon surfacing you find that the surf is considerably larger than when you began your dive, oh well, you're on your own and you'd better be capable of negotiating you way through it – without a buddy to hold your hand. Or perhaps on the way back to the boat you discover that the current is a bit stronger than expected (although this, like the former example, should have been factored into your dive plan). At this point, you'd better be sure of your physical stamina and swimming abilities because you won't have a buddy to rely on for a tow.

Solo diving requires that a diver be capable of fending for him/ herself and not be buddy-dependent.

Clearly, the above scenarios, as well as a host of additional situations, require a diver to know his/her physical limitations and to stay within those limitations *(see Chapter 4)*. But, how can you ascertain what your limitations are and what can be done to extend them?

Defining your limitations is a matter of first knowing your strengths and weaknesses. Are you a strong swimmer? How developed are your free diving abilities? Is your training and experience conducive with whatever type of diving you're considering? The list could continue *ad infinitum*. What's important is that you tailor it to fit your individual needs and dive requirements, remember to take into account all of the influencing environmental factors: (surf, surge, current, kelp, rocky entry/exit, etc.). As discussed in

Chapter 2, self-evaluation and self-regulation are crucial to safety. If your knowledge and experience do not reflect the necessary prerequisites for a particular dive, pursue additional training from a qualified instructor. If it's your physical abilities (i.e. level of fitness) that concern you, get in shape before you enter into this type of diving. *(Keep in mind that before diving any new location or entering into any new type of diving, it may be prudent to first dive with a competent, self-sufficient diver who is better qualified and experienced. It is usually not sufficient, or wise, to rely on information gained from reading or verbal instruction in lieu of actually diving with a qualified buddy.)*

I realize that "getting in shape" for some divers is easier said than done. It is, however, as critical (perhaps more so) a factor as self-evaluation and regulation. This is a book about solo diving, not fitness and exercise. Therefore if you would like further, detailed information about individual fitness programs I recommend that you seek the advice of a professional athletic trainer or any of several excellent books on the subject *(See Reference Materials)*. Also, before entering into a fitness program, especially if you are over 30, be sure to get a complete medical examination.

Following are a couple select exercise suggestions that, if applied on a regular basis, will aid you along the road to self-sufficiency. These are not meant to be complete fitness programs. They are to be used in conjunction with whatever type of program you choose. Keep in mind that any exercise activity should be carried on at least every other day, and should last for a minimum of 20 minutes. Anything less than this would result in a minimal amount of benefit. However, any exercise is better than none.

Swimming

Since scuba diving is an activity that takes place in water, it makes sense that exercises that are water-specific (conducted in water) would be most appropriate. The most obvious form of water-related exercise is swimming (and I don't mean floating around the pool with a martini in one hand and a cigarette in the other). Swimming is an endurance activity, and has long been noted for its cardiovascular (pertaining to the heart and blood vessels) benefits; and as far as divers are concerned, this is vitally important. Increased cardiovascular fitness will help to reduce fatigue (better endurance), lower your air-consumption rate (increased bottom time!), and, as new research is indicating, possibly decrease your susceptibility to nitrogen narcosis. Swimming also increases stamina and aerobic capacity; thus providing the diver with an additional edge for safety.

It has been said that due to all the modern equipment used by today's sport divers, a person doesn't have to know how to swim. In my opinion, that's analogous to telling someone that eyesight isn't required to fly an airplane. I sincerely believe that an individual desiring to scuba dive first possess good or better swimming abilities. That doesn't mean that all good swimmers make good divers. However, you would be hard-pressed to find a competent, self-sufficient diver who isn't a good swimmer as well.

If you're not fortunate enough to have a swimming pool in your backyard, there's probably a local YMCA or health club in your area that can be used. Additionally, if you live relatively close to the area that you normally dive, this too might prove to be a good location for swimming. If it is, it would also give you an opportunity to spend more time in this environment (*see my comments on this below*).

Free, Skin, and Breath-hold Diving

Another excellent form of exercise that is water-specific and closely related to scuba diving is free diving (a.k.a. skin diving or breath-hold diving).

Free diving, like swimming, can also be classified as an endurance activity. It involves various types of basic equipment that may vary from one geographic location (or individual) to another. The equipment consists of at least a mask and fins, but may include a wetsuit and/or drysuit, booties (depending on the type of fins used), minimal weight if desired, and snorkel (although some free diving enthusiasts would argue that true free divers don't use snorkels). I have also on occasion included a BCD as part of my gear (this too could be sacrilege).

The benefits of free diving are very similar to those provided by swimming. Not only are some of the same muscles utilized, but free diving takes place in the same water environment that you scuba dive in, whereas swimming is normally done in a pool. The benefits of free diving in the same location that you scuba dive are three-fold. You're not only engaging in a form of exercise that allows you to increase your aerobic capacity, but it also allows you to become more familiar with a particular location; which ultimately makes you more comfortable scuba diving at that location. Thirdly, the object of breath-hold diving for exercise is to gradually increase the depth to which you can dive (within safe limits, of course). This builds upon a diver's psychological fitness (confidence, being comfortable in the water, technique, etc.) and contributes to the overall competence and self-sufficiency of the individual which, as we have seen, are all very important factors for the solo diver.

The above activities are highly recommended for divers because of the host of benefits that can be accrued from their inclusion to any fitness program. They not only provide for the diver increased cardiovascular fitness, but increased aerobic capacity as well. In the October 1990 edition of **Discover Diving** magazine, columnist Eric Hanauer related the following:

Fitness has several components, including strength, speed, flexibility, and aerobic capacity. Among them, aerobic capacity is the most important for divers. This is what keeps you going on hard swims, through the surf, against strong currents, or on long surface swims back to the boat when you have misjudged the duration of your air supply. Generally speaking, any exercise lasting 45 seconds or more draws on your aerobic capacity. Quick sprints of less than that duration are classified as anaerobic. Since most diving activities last longer than 45 seconds, endurance is far more important than speed in our activity.

Endurance improves whenever you raise your pulse rate to 80% of maximum, and keep it there for 20 minutes or more. This may be accomplished through running, swimming, aerobics, bicycling, or anything that keeps you moving at a steady pace. Recommended maximum pulse rate is determined by the formula of 220 minus your age. Therefore, recommended maximum for a 30 year-old would be 190, and 80% of that is 152. Remember, these are general recommendations, and individuals vary in their reaction to cardiac stress.

Bad Habits vs. Safe Diving

This is the part of the chapter where you'll probably need that drink that I eluded to above. And on second thought, instead of a strong one, make it non-alcoholic. After all, we are discussing physical fitness.

As solo divers, it's vitally important that we follow certain safety guidelines, and in addition to the ones reviewed in Chapter 4, there are a few that specifically apply to physical fitness and physiology. The guidelines that I'm referring to are perhaps better known as common sense, for they are connected with habits, bad habits. As such they become, in this author's opinion, definite contraindications to solo diving. For the sake of convenience, I have placed these contraindications in the form of problems in table 3.1. Along with each problem is its associated cause (omitted if obvious), a sample of the negative effects related to each problem, and a solution. The table is not meant to be all-inclusive. There are various other problems that I have chosen not to address as well as a plethora of additional negative effects surrounding each problem. The solutions listed are the most obvious and may not apply to all individuals.

The problems addressed in Table 3.1 are a selection of the most obvious and prevalent contraindications. There are certainly going to be exceptions to every case, but just how far should an individual go before drawing the line and deciding to either correct the problem or stop diving. The solo diver needs to be in excellent physical shape in order to perform safely and adeptly in the underwater environment. I'm sure that there will be a few divers who read this information and will say to themselves, "Well, I smoke and I'm a few pounds overweight, but what the hell, I'm a very capable diver anyway. So I guess this doesn't really apply to me." Guess again. Smoking, drug use, alcohol abuse, and high levels of stress are most certainly and without a doubt solid contraindications to scuba diving in any form, solo or not. And when it comes to obesity, that's a judgement call – one that can be better answered by yourself and a physician (preferably one who is familiar with the physics and demands of diving). If you're slightly overweight, a condition that unfortunately describes

The solo diver needs to be in excellent physical shape in order to perform safely and adeptly in the underwater environment.

Photo by Tab Brewer

Table 3.1

Contraindications to Scuba Diving

Problem	Cause	Negative Diving-Related Effects	Solution
Smoking	–	Decreased cardio-vascular fitness; loss of aerobic capacity; decreased stamina; decreased pulmonary fitness	Stop smoking
Obesity	Overeating & assoc. problems	Decreased cardio-vascular fitness; decreased stamina; increased chance of heat exhaustion; less efficient out-gassing of nitrogen	Diet; exercise; seek the advice of a physician
Alcohol Abuse	–	Increases blood circulation to skin, thus increasing loss of body heat; contributes to dehydration; increases suseptibility to nitrogen narcosis and decompression sickness	Limit alcohol consumption; seek the advice of a physician if necessary
Drug Abuse	–	Depending on the drug(s), use in connection with scuba diving could be fatal	Seek the advice of a physician
Stress	Causes vary with each individual; may be work- or family-related	Due to various physiological changes that occur when a diver is over-stressed, each varying individually, the person in question could be more susceptible to a number of diving related maladies; contributes to less awareness of surroundings and important safety factors.	Learn to control stress; seek the advice of a physician if necessary

most of the diving community, then perhaps you'll not have a problem. But anything other than a few extra pounds can present a prime situation for disaster. In all the years that I've been teaching, the single most influential factor that has been responsible for keeping students from scuba diving is obesity. As you can see in the table, it decreases two of the most important physiological factors inherent in good, safe diving – cardiovascular fitness and stamina. In fact, the two go hand-in-hand. If your cardiovascular fitness levels are low, then you can bet that your stamina will be much less than optimal.

So, now that your almost done with this chapter and getting ready to polish off a box of *Screaming Yellow Zonkers* and a six-pack of *Budweiser*, perhaps it would be wise to reach for the cottage cheese and orange juice instead. And while you're at it, thumb through the Yellow Pages and see if you can locate a health club that's close to home. You'll not only be a better solo diver (or any kind of diver for that matter), but you'll be a lot safer down there as well.

In Chapter 4 we'll be taking a look at Dive Management Guidelines that include a host of planning procedures designed to make solo diving a safe and enjoyable experience. These guidelines, if used in conjunction with the other material contained in this text, will increase the solo diver's ability to enter the underwater realm as a self-sufficient, proficient diver and be able to prevent emergencies before they have a chance to occur.

Chapter 4

Dive Management Guidelines

The sea rarely offers us more than one chance. Should we foolishly fall into error, the outcome is all too obvious. By its very nature, the sea cannot choose favorites – they are chosen by themselves through wise decision and hard-learned knowledge. It is often the small, overlooked details that, to the discerning mind, become the dividing line between success and outright failure.

John David Roberts

It has long been an axiom of mine that the little things are infinitely the most important.

Sherlock Holmes

The Ostrich Syndrome

As an advocate of solo diving I have on occasion been asked the question "How can you as an instructor condone an activity that isn't officially sanctioned by the sport diving industry?" After I stop laughing, I regain my composure and reply with a quote from Bob Dylan: *"If you live outside the law you must be honest."* This usually requires a bit of elucidation. The law as it pertains to sport diving isn't always clear-cut, nor is it always valid. According to this law I'm not supposed to dive solo (although the reasons given are somewhat ambiguous). Therefore as a solo diver I'm living outside the law. By authoring this book I'm addressing an issue that needs enlightenment. This is my way of being honest.

The sport diving industry at present (at least some facets of it) suffers from an ailment that I've termed "the ostrich syndrome." When an ostrich senses any sign of trouble or trepidation it immediately buries its head in the sand, a rather unbecoming posture that many so-called "leaders" in the sport diving community have assumed in connection with the issue of solo diving. Because of this unproductive position, those divers who have elected to go solo have found it nearly impossible to access up-to-date information that applies to their chosen style of diving.

In this chapter I have taken a number of select guidelines and informational concepts and ordered them into mini sub-chapters each dealing with their respective subjects. Although many of them are unrelated, they all have one common objective - diver safety. They are, as the chapter title suggests, **Dive Management Guidelines** that are intended to enhance and amplify a diver's level of self-sufficiency. They're recommended for solo diving but are certainly compatible with buddy diving as well.

Dive Planning Rules

Scuba diving, particularly when done alone, has a host of rules that need to be heeded. We all remember the ubiquitous axiom "always breathe," or the equally important "never ascend faster than your smallest bubbles." These are, or should be, fundamental basics learned by all divers in the initial stages of their Open Water/Entry Level course. The two rules that are presented and discussed below are not as widely known. But once understood, their importance becomes just as obvious. They are safety considerations that should be factored into every dive - especially when going solo.

Keep in mind that these "rules" are not carved in stone and are to be used as guidelines. There are obvious exceptions to them such as cave diving, wreck diving, and deep diving (all types of diving that, in the eyes of some, may be best conducted with a competent, experienced, self-sufficient buddy), and it is each diver's responsibility to decide what's appropriate and prudent for him/her.

Rule #1
Never scuba dive deeper than twice the depth to which you can free dive.

Rule #2
A diver's underwater distance from the point of exit (shore, boat, etc.) should not exceed the distance that they can comfortably and easily swim, equipped with full scuba gear, on the surface.

If we refer back to Chapter 3 and our definition of fit, we can see how these tenets apply. By staying within the suggested parameters a diver would provide a good degree of safety for him/herself. Allow me to elucidate a bit further on the two rules and dissect them for the purpose of understanding.

Rule #1 tells us that we should limit our sport diving depth to no more than twice the depth to which we can free dive. Now, for many of you this literally means that you shouldn't scuba dive much deeper than 30 feet (9m), or perhaps less. As I've already stated, these rules are included here as general guidelines. However, don't push your true limits. The key word is "true". I'm a firm believer in the value of physical fitness, and for some of you, 30 feet may indeed be your true, safe limit - with or without a buddy. Need I remind you that just because you possess a certification card (or a copy of this book) doesn't mean that you're automatically competent to dive alone to even 30 feet. Unfortunately, c-cards are like driver's licenses; lots of people have them that shouldn't.

I know what you're thinking: "My instructor taught me that the sport diving limit is 130 fsw. They never said anything about twice my free diving limit...blah blah." That's entirely understandable; they probably aren't familiar with the concept. And according to most diving texts, what they taught you is absolutely correct. But then again, most diving texts still tell you that you're safer with a buddy.

Staying within the depth limitations described by Rule #1 has some obvious safety benefits. Should a diver encounter an out-of-air situation, they may find it necessary to perform an emergency swimming ascent (ESA). If they're within twice their free diving limit, the chances of the ESA being performed safely and without incident are greatly increased. Additionally, a diver within these limits will feel more mentally competent (an often overlooked, key ingredient in diver safety) when making the dive.

Photo by Ken Loyst

I have always taught my students that one's competency and proficiency as a self-sufficient scuba diver are directly proportional to one's free diving abilities. Plainly stated, a good breath-hold diver has a better chance of becoming a competent scuba diver than a person whose free diving skills are lacking.

Although I plainly understand that a good thing can be taken too far, where safety and common sense are concerned, how far is too far? With a little effort and determination one's free diving skill level can be effectively increased. Not only will this add to your abilities as a scuba diver, but the exercise and physical conditioning that are a part of this effort make it all the more worthwhile. You ultimately make the decision for how deep you dive. But if you're diving solo, a little extra precaution goes a long way.

Now let's take a look at Rule #2 which states that a diver's underwater distance from his/her point of exit should not exceed the distance that they can comfortably and easily swim, fully equipped with scuba gear, on the surface. This again is another safety recommendation with which you may not be familiar. Nevertheless, it is an excellent guideline that is especially appropriate for solo divers.

If a diver should encounter a problem either underwater or on the surface they may find it necessary, or even imperative, to exit the water sooner than planned. Depending upon the degree of urgency, and taking into account the fact that there isn't a buddy present to assist, they would not want to be farther from the point of exit than they can safely swim. If they are farther away than Rule #2 prescribes, they may run out of strength before they run out of water. *(Adherence to this rule does not insure that the diver will safely get to the point of exit. It does, however, add a degree of safety that shouldn't be overlooked.)*

Now, in order to stay within the parameters of Rule #2 there are a few considerations that should first be addressed. Most importantly, are your navigational skills sufficient enough to keep you in proper position relative to the exit? Have you accounted for any current and/or surge and the course deviation that they may affect? Is this going to be a particularly arduous dive - one that would require more energy (physical or mental) than is usually necessary? Are you sufficiently familiar with this location, or would it be prudent to include a more qualified buddy who has additional experience diving this site?

A diver's underwater distance from his/her point of exit should not exceed the distance that they can comfortably and easily swim, fully equipped with scuba gear, on the surface.

As one can see, Rule #2 requires a lot more planning and preparation than Rule #1. However, it is a safety guideline that should be implemented when diving alone. And when followed accordingly, the benefits are well worth the effort.

Let me remind you again that these rules are guidelines, and as such may need to be amended in one form or another to meet the particular requirements of a dive. This may mean either more conservative or liberal compliance with their limits, or the complete eradication thereof. Whatever the choice, safety is the most important consideration.

Air Management

Like the old saying goes, we're "creatures of habit." If this is true, then I would venture to guess that a majority of our habits could most likely be disposed of, with, of course, the exception of one – breathing. If not for our need to breathe, bottom time would take on a whole new meaning. But since we happen to be saddled with this physiological curse, we're left with the alternative - air management.

For many divers, air management means keeping an eye on their pressure gauge (SPG) and ascending when they're down to 500 psi. Well, that's not exactly what I had in mind. As I've reiterated throughout this text, solo diving requires efficient planning and

Photo courtesy Underwater Kinetics

preparation beyond what is generally taught in most scuba courses, and an integral part of that planning involves our air and how we manage it.

As we can see in table 4.1, air is made up of several components or gasses with nitrogen accounting for approximately 78% of the mix and oxygen roughly 21%.

Commercial diving sometimes involves a mix other than air and requires specialized training and instruction over and above what is taught in a conventional scuba class.

Table 4.1

Gas	Percentage by Volume
Nitrogen	78.084
Oxygen	20.946
Argon	.934
Carbon Dioxide	.033
Rare Gases	.003

Composition of Air in It's Natural State

The residual, approximately 1%, is composed of argon, carbon dioxide, and an assortment of rare gases.

Since air is a mixture of gases, this means that technically all dives are made on mixed gas, with air being the most common mix used. There are also various other mixes in use for sport diving such as Nitrox and Tri-mix. Any diving that involves a mix other than air requires specialized training and instruction over and above what is taught in a conventional scuba class and unfortunately, the scope of this book doesn't allow for their discussion. However, their use by sport divers as well as the research and commercial facets of the industry is gradually becoming more commonplace. These and other mixes may in fact one day replace air as the standard for many levels of diving.

For now, with air as the mixed gas of choice, it is important to not only monitor how much of it we have left during the course of a dive, but even before entering the water it is imperative that, as solo divers, we establish a few rules of the road.

Different types of diving means different types of air management. Cave divers use the "Rule of Thirds." It states that when 1/3 of a diver's air supply has been exhausted, it's time to turn back so that an additional 1/3 will be available to exit the cave. The remaining 1/3 is used for the ascent.

Wreck divers also have their own philosophies about air management. It can be summed-up in one word – redundancy. Cathie Cush, a free-lance writer and experienced east coast wreck diver

Research diving, like other forms of advanced, specialized diving, requires special air management guidelines.

Photo by Darren Webb

addressed the concern of redundancy quite well in the second issue of **AquaCorps: The Journal for Experienced Divers.**

If a dozen divers descend any given anchor line to a mid-Atlantic wreck, you can bet you'll see a dozen different air systems in action. Singles, doubles, old steel 72s, new high-pressure cylinders, pony bottles, manifolds, cheater bars... you get the picture.

About the only thing divers around here agree on is that when it comes to air, the more the better.

One reason for the variety is the sites we encounter off the northeast coast. A set-up that might work fine on an 80-foot lobster dive would be dangerously inadequate on a 130-foot shipwreck. A penetration at 220 feet requires something else again – and usually a rig you probably don't want to lug around if it's not absolutely necessary.

In addition to cave and wreck divers, search and rescue teams, military divers, researchers, and commercial divers all have their own set of air supply management rules that they too abide by. So, depending on your choice of diving, it would behoove you to contact other divers who are expert in their field and ask what is recommended. *(See Reference Materials for information about various specialty organizations.)*

The air management guidelines included in this chapter are for dives that do not include cave, cavern, or wreck penetration, deep diving, or any other type of specialty diving that would involve high-risk activity. As I've stated in previous chapters, common sense is the watchword and when necessary, seek further training and instruction before involving yourself in a situation that you are ill-prepared for.

Air supply redundancy is a very important consideration not only for cave and wreck diving, but for solo diving as well. Since there isn't a buddy to rely on for emergency air (a practice that is less than desirable anyway), it's imperative that you have an emergency back-up system of your own. I've relegated the issue of redundancy to Chapter 5 where I discuss in detail the various systems currently available as well as how to use them.

Air management for solo divers is of tremendous importance. It isn't enough to follow basic guidelines and hope that they'll be sufficient. They aren't. It's not only necessary to monitor your air

Table 4.2

Depth vs. Minimum Cylinder Pressure on Ascent

Depth in Feet[1]	Minimum psi at Beginning of Ascent
0-50	500
51-60	600
61-70	700
71-80	800
81-90	900
91-100	1000
101-110	1100
111-120	1200
121-130	1300
131-140	1400
141-150	1500

[1]To convert from feet to meters use the following conversion: ft/3.3=meters

supply, but it's equally critical to know when to ascend and with how much air remaining in your cylinder.

Table 4.2 illustrates just how much air should be reserved for the ascent phase of a dive. It is suggested that the minimums listed in column two be followed without exception and may be increased if it would be prudent to do so (cold water, arduous activity, heavy surge, strong current, large surf, etc.). The limits for minimum psi apply no matter what size cylinder is used.

The figures on Table 4.2 are derived from taking the planned maximum depth and rounding up to the next highest power of ten (unless of course the depth happens to be exactly 50', 60', 70', etc.) and adding a zero. This would realistically allow the diver plenty of air to ascend at the prescribed ascent rate of 60 feet-per-minute and still have enough air to make a safety stop. *(See Ascents below for further information about safety stops.)*

Air Consumption

As a diving instructor, one of the most common questions that I'm asked is "How can I increase my bottom time?". This is like asking someone to explain Einstein's theory of relativity. You'd better have a lot of time and plenty of paper with which to take notes.

Although I realize that bottom time and relativity have little in common, I would like to point out that maximizing your bottom time can be more complex than it would first appear. It doesn't have to be complicated, but there are a number of elements that need to be factored in, and depending on the individual and type of diving to be conducted, more than one could be involved.

More dive time means less air consumption; and to consume less air requires a number of things:

1) Proper physical fitness
2) Efficient breathing control
3) Proper weighting
4) Efficient buoyancy control.

Any one of these factors can play an important part in air consumption and ultimately affect your bottom time. Let's now examine each one to determine how to extend your air supply and increase your dive time.

Since the topic of physical fitness was previously addressed in Chapter 3, we'll continue on to the question of **Efficient Breathing Control**.

As you probably remember from your open water course, the proper breathing pattern is a deep inhalation followed by a slow, balanced exhalation. Shallow breathing doesn't allow for proper air exchange in the lungs, so only a minimal amount of CO_2 is eliminated with each breath. An increased amount of CO_2 in the lungs means that less can diffuse out of the blood into the lungs. An increased amount of CO_2 in the blood (hypercapnia) will create a greater desire to breathe. Increased breathing means more air will be consumed at a faster pace, all of which means less bottom time.

Conversely, breathing much deeper and more rapidly than desirable is called hyperventilation and has an opposite physiological effect on the diver than shallow breathing. With hyperventilation the CO_2 level in the lungs is severely reduced, and if continued, will be lowered below normal levels. Since CO_2 provides the physiological stimulus to breathe, the diver will feel less need to breathe following hyperventilation. This process can eventually lead to an overall decrease in the available oxygen (hypoxia), thus unconsciousness due to oxygen deficiency could result without warning. Need I explain how unconsciousness would effect bottom time?

Another method of breathing that is practiced is called skip-breathing. This involves holding each breath for as long as possible before taking another. Many divers believe that this will conserve air when in fact, quite the opposite is true. Skip-breathing is not advised because it results in the buildup of excess CO_2 in the system (hypercapnia) and can easily lead to overexertion. (It also breaks one of the fundamental rules of scuba diving, breathe continuously.) If a diver becomes overexerted, he/she will consume more of their air supply and once again the result will be less bottom time.

So remember, maintain an efficient pattern of breathing (deep inhalation; slow, balanced exhalation) and watch your air consumption decrease while your bottom time increases.

Another factor influencing air consumption is proper weighting. This is definitely one area where more isn't better. If a diver is overweighted, the consequences are obvious: overexertion, less efficient buoyancy control, increased air consumption, and ultimately less dive time. Also, I have seen overweighted divers who found it difficult to ascend at the end of their dive, and due to this unexpected dilemma, became apprehensive (one of the first stages of panic) and required assistance to ascend safely. This not only presented a direct threat to their safety, but to the rescuer as well.

(Allow me to point out the all-too-obvious fact that this is just the type of individual that should definitely not be solo diving, and perhaps should avoid diving altogether until they have at least received further instruction.)

Efficient buoyancy control also contributes to a more efficient use of the air supply. Again, referring back to your basic open water course, neutral buoyancy is the desired state of buoyancy for a diver. Considering the fact that this isn't a text for beginning divers, I'll not take the time to explain how to achieve neutral buoyancy. But I would like to point out that if a diver is relatively stable in the water (neutral), the need to constantly inflate and deflate the BCD is eradicated. Since inflating and deflating both rapidly deplete a diver's air supply, it stands to reason that if this process is eliminated, more air will be conserved for other purposes. Additionally, when the diver is neutral it allows him/her to stay at a given depth and not have to move up and down in the water column, thus conserving energy which in turn conserves air.

I'd like to bring attention to the fact that the terms positive, neutral, and negative as used above in reference to buoyancy are really misnomers. Buoyancy, like gravity, is a vector quantity, and just as gravity is a force of attraction by which terrestrial objects tend to fall toward the center of the earth (downward), buoyancy is an upward pressure exerted by a fluid in which an object is immersed. Therefore to say that something is positively, neutrally, or negatively buoyant is technically incorrect.

Thermal Protection

Another area of concern when it comes to air consumption is thermal protection. It is also an important factor in dive planning. If a diver is overheated or too cold the ramifications can certainly be less than desirable and could prove to be life-threatening if left unchecked. Below is a brief synopsis of various thermal protection-related concerns and a few of their associated problems. I've also included a few solutions that may be helpful.

The connection between thermal protection and air consumption stems from the fact that if a diver isn't properly outfitted they will be uncomfortable and in turn will deplete more of their air supply than necessary. A majority of my diving is done off the west coast of the United States where the water temperature requires a certain degree of thermal protection. If you dive this area regularly you're aware of

Photos courtesy Diving Unlimited International, Inc.

Dry suits and underwear are occasionally warranted depending on the environment and/or diver preference.

the requirements. However, I've seen many divers from other parts of the country (or from other countries) who weren't aware of these considerations and, much to their surprise, acquired a quick lesson in thermal protection. Not only were they less than comfortable (to say the least), but their air consumption reflected their ignorance. Now, after all you "true" cold water divers stop laughing (California isn't really cold water diving, unless of course you're used to warmer waters), I would like to bring attention to the fact that even in water that is 80°F (26°C), some form of thermal protection should still be worn. It not only keeps you warm, but protects you from cuts, scrapes, and abrasions as well.

Prolonged exposure to cold water can lead to hypothermia, a condition in which the deep tissue or core temperature of the body falls below the normal physiological range (approximately 97°F or 36°C), and is the temperature at which physiological malfunctions occur. If the core temperature continues to drop, the consequences could prove to be fatal. Conversely, if a diver gets overheated it can lead to heat exhaustion and, in extreme cases, heat stroke; both of which can be dangerous.

Proper thermal protection is dictated primarily by environmental conditions and should be factored into your dive planning well in advance of making the dive. If you're not familiar with a particular area or region, be sure to find out what type of protection is necessary before jumping into the water; you might just save yourself one of those proverbial hard-learned lessons.

Air Consumption Calculations

An additional aspect of air management involves being able to ascertain how much air you consume in terms of psi/minute. Armed with this information, you can graphically analyze your breathing efficiency (or lack thereof) as well as determine how long you can safely remain at depth.

The formula for calculating your surface air consumption rate (SAC rate) is as follows:

SAC rate = (ac/bt) / (d+33/33)

ac = air consumed (psi)
bt = bottom time (minutes)
d = depth (feet)

Sample problem: If a diver spends 40 minutes at a depth of 60 feet (18.2m), makes a three minute safety stop at 20 feet (6.1m), and uses a total of 2500 psi, what would the diver's surface air consumption rate be?

Solution: (2500psi/43min.) / (60ft+33/33) = 20.7 psi/min.

Once you've determined your SAC rate you can then concentrate on lowering it, thereby increasing your dive time. As I stated earlier, these calculations can also be utilized to determine how long you can remain at a particular depth. Keep in mind that your SAC rate, as determined, using a tank of one size, will probably not work for planning purposes if a tank of a different size is used. In this case, it would be necessary to recalculate for the new tank size.

Ascents

A recent survey showed that a majority of divers do not make a safety stop before surfacing even though doing so greatly reduces the risk of nitrogen bubble formation. To put it in plain English, less chance of getting bent.

In September of 1989 the American Academy of Underwater Sciences (AAUS) sponsored a workshop in Woods Hole, Massachusetts titled *Biomechanics of Safe Ascents*. Present at the workshop were experts in many diving-related fields such as hyperbaric medicine and decompression theory. The AAUS concluded that a 3-5 minute stop between 10 and 30 feet is significantly more effective at preventing and eliminating "silent bubbles" than a slower ascent rate of 20-40 ft/min. and no stop. The silent bubbles are believed to be the precursors of decompression sickness.

I teach just such a procedure to my Entry Level/Open Water students. They know it as S.O.A.P., the Safety Outgassing Ascent Procedure. It is technically a decompression stop, and that's exactly what it is designed for. Now, you may be thinking "I follow my dive tables and avoid decompression diving, therefore I don't need to make a safety stop." Well, you may indeed stick to your tables, but I have news for you: Every dive is a decompression dive. Decompression simply means outgassing, the outgassing of nitrogen that has been accumulated from diving, even if that diving has been within the limits specified by your tables. So, for safety's sake, make a stop at the top (10-30ft/3-5min.) at the end of every dive.

Cold H$_2$O/Arduous Dive Variation

In addition to the dive management guidelines that I've discussed above, I'd like to offer one other consideration that, as a solo diver, you might wish to include in your dive plans.

The Cold H$_2$O/Arduous Dive Variation is an extra safety precaution that I automatically build into any dive profile that applies. It requires the deduction of five minutes off the no-stop limits (i.e. no-decompression limits, maximum dive time) for any dive that is made in cold water. For me, cold water is defined as water colder than 55°F or 12.8°C, although this may vary from one individual to the next depending on the temperature of water you're accustomed to diving in. It also requires a five minute no-stop deduction if the dive involves activity that is more arduous (energy consuming) than normal. Again, one diver's definition of arduous may not be the same as another's. If the dive involves both cold water and arduous activity, then a total of 10 minutes should be deducted.

The purpose of this variation is two-fold: A) In cold water, your body doesn't outgas the excess, accumulated nitrogen quite as efficiently as it normally would. B) During arduous underwater activity, more nitrogen than normal will be accumulated (ingassed) due to the increased breathing rate as well as other physiological changes that come into play. The 5 or 10 minute deduction simply keeps the diver from diving too close to the edge of the tables.

Considering the fact that many tables now available have already decreased the no-stop limits, the Cold H_2O/Arduous Dive Variation may not need to be implemented if one of these tables is used. Additionally, when using a dive computer the variation may not be necessary. However, this will depend on the model of dive computer used as well as the type of diving to be performed.

In Chapter 5 we will examine various types of emergency breathing systems currently available, their use, and how they apply to self-rescue.

Chapter 5

Emergency Breathing Systems & Self-Rescue

We live in a gear-driven culture and techno-breakdowns confront us in nearly every aspect of modern life. In most cases, planning problems and equipment failures are just an inconvenience; in diving they often mean death.

Michael Menduno

Proper prior planning prevents poor performance. (Affectionately known as the rule of six P's.)

Anonymous

Your most important piece of diving equipment is a free and clear head.

Carlos Eyles

Out of Air

I've never had the displeasure of running out of air. Do I consider myself lucky? No, I don't think luck has anything to do with it; it's a matter of discipline. I constantly check and recheck my gauges. I also strictly adhere to the guidelines outlined in Chapter 4, Table 4.2. I'm aware of the fact that there are those rare occasions when a diver's equipment malfunctions and all the discipline in the world won't do a damn thing to prevent it. So in that sense I guess I have been lucky. But aside from spontaneous gear failure (most of which can be prevented by regular maintenance), I still contend that running out of air is like running out of gasoline; it can be prevented by monitoring one's gauges. So why write an entire chapter about Emergency Breathing Systems and Self-Rescue if avoiding an out-of-air situation is as simple as monitoring your SPG and keeping your equipment well-maintained? The answer requires a two-fold response: 1) As I've eluded to above, accidents can happen to even the most diligent, careful divers. 2) Knowledge, as the old saying goes, is power; and in this case that power can be applied to prevention.

Most of you were probably taught that when an out-of-air emergency occurs you should seek the assistance of your buddy – if they happen to be close enough to be able to render assistance. If they're not close enough, go to plan "B"– an emergency swimming ascent (emergency out-of-air ascent).

In the case of your buddy assisting you (sharing air ascent), he/she would give you their octopus (safe-second) and you would then ascend while holding onto each other. Upon surfacing, you would manually inflate your BCD, apologize for being foolish enough to run out of air, and then swim back to your point of exit. Sounds easy enough. In fact, you even practiced it in the pool and again in the open water and it didn't seem too complicated. But remember, these were controlled scenarios where an instructor or divemaster was standing by. Add in a touch of reality, a bit of panic, 60+ feet of water, and the fact that you haven't practiced it recently (never with this particular buddy) and it doesn't seem quite so easy anymore. Some researchers report that in as many as 50% of out-of-air incidents analyzed, the victim's buddy was either unwilling or unable to assist *(See Dr. E. Thalman, "Diving Systems Stimulate Discussion," Pressure, July/August 1989).*

In the case of an emergency swimming ascent (ESA), you were told to spit out your regulator (some of you were probably taught to retain it, depending on your instructor and certification agency), hyperextend your airway (look up or tilt your head back), exhale continuously upon ascent, flare-out near the top, and hope for the best. Now, if you were fortunate enough not to incur a lung overexpansion injury or miss a decompression stop, you could then go on your merry way and promise yourself never to run out of air again. Perhaps I'm a bit too cynical, but for scme reason I always thought that there had to be a better way. I don't believe in relying on my buddy for anything, especially my air supply, and an ESA seemed a little too risky.

The above scenarios don't take into account rough-water conditions or overhead environments (wrecks, caves, ice, etc.) and they

But what about the solo diver? Since there's no buddy available and an ESA isn't a wise choice for a back-up plan, what options are available and how do they apply to various types of diving?

Photo by Darren Webb

don't properly address the issue of the solo diver and what options he/she has available (surely an ESA is not an acceptable option for solo diving). I have also not yet mentioned buddy-breathing; this is when two divers share one second stage regulator and ascend while taking turns breathing. In case you're not aware of the facts, buddy-breathing has been responsible for numerous double drownings and is no longer recognized or taught as a viable out-of-air option (unless of course the instructor in question has been living in a cave). In fact, some instructors teach that you'd be better off performing an ESA than attempting to buddy-breathe, and judging from my experience, their logic seems to make sense.

But what about the solo diver? Since there's no buddy available and an ESA isn't a wise choice for a back-up plan, what options are available and how do they apply to various types of diving?

In the rest of this chapter I've dealt with several emergency breathing systems (EBS) and how they're commonly used as well as what applications they have. Note that specialty types of diving such as wreck diving, cave diving, ice and deep diving, etc., all have particular requirements that must be met in order to comply with accepted safety standards. Obviously, there aren't any scuba police and no one can force you to comply with the standards. But as solo divers, these standards take on a whole new importance and non-compliance, aside from being foolish, takes away a vital safety edge that all too often is needed. I've divided the various systems into two basic categories: Type I (Alternate Air Supply) and Type II (Redundant Air Supply). Both categories vary greatly in their respective applications as well as the type of out-of-air coverage they supply.

TYPE I: ALTERNATE AIR SUPPLY

Type I emergency breathing systems are very different from Type II in that they do not offer air supply redundancy. However, they do offer one form of redundancy – a back-up second stage regulator. Due to the fact that they don't provide an additional air supply, I refer to them as alternates. Their primary function in the recreational diving community is one of supplying an out-of-air buddy with an octopus/safe-second, or in the case of a primary second-stage failure, to supply the diver with an emergency back-up. For solo diving, Type I systems are excellent as second-stage back-ups, but they are by no means adequate without at least some form of

Type II system. This is obviously because of their lack of redundancy – a factor that is to solo diving what a parachute is to fighter pilots. If, as a solo diver, you should experience an out-of-air emergency and were not supplied with a Type II EBS, the only other option (except drowning) is an emergency swimming ascent, and this, as we have already seen, is not desirable.

We will now examine various Type I systems that are currently available. Pay particular attention to how they are connected or attached to the diver as well as each unit's functionality.

Octopus/Safe-Second

This is perhaps the most widely used of all the Type I systems and depending on how you were taught and from which certification agency, you may know it by one or more names: octopus, bipus regulator, safe-second, etc. Different names, same purpose. Every major diving equipment manufacturer has at least one style octopus available. As one would expect, they are available in a variety of colors, but since they're emergency units, the most widely used colors are yellow, orange, or bright red. However, with the advent of the day-glo and fluorescent colors such as pink and lime green, visibility (of the EBS) takes on new meaning.

Positioning of the octopus is anything but standardized. For the most part, I have always taught my students that the only piece of equipment over their right shoulder should be their primary second-stage, everything else (gauges, low pressure inflator hose(s), and octopus) should be on their left side. This type of gear configuration is certainly not universal and depending on your own preference, it may differ substantially. One key point to keep in mind is to be sure that none of your equipment, particularly the EBS, is dangling free where it can get tangled or damaged. One of my former students who went on to become an instructor told me that on the only occasion when he needed his octopus (fortunately it wasn't a life-threatening situation) he discovered that it had been dragging on the bottom and was so full of sand that it was useless. Needless to say, he now keeps it in a more secure position.

The typical octopus looks identical to a primary second-stage (often it is the same regulator with a different colored case); some models however are slightly different internally and others have the option of being either a right- or left-handed unit.

The disadvantages of an octopus as opposed to the remaining Type I units discussed here are more personal than technical. An octopus requires another low-pressure hose, whereas the other units are integrated into the power inflator on the buoyancy compensator. This in turn means not only more bulk, but more drag as well. Also, as mentioned above, some type of retaining device or special pocket is necessary to keep the regulator from dragging along the bottom and into rocks, kelp, coral, etc.

Scubapro **A.I.R. 2**

In 1979 Scubapro introduced the A.I.R. 2 (Alternate Inflation Regulator) to the diving industry. It was the first unit of its kind to incorporate a safe-second into the power inflator. With this new innovation, the power inflator and safe-second stage were combined together in one body, thus eliminating the need for an additional low-pressure hose that was previously necessary for an octopus.

One of the main advantages to this type of safe-second/power inflator EBS is the location of the unit. It is designed for left-hand use and is always positioned at the end of the BCD inflator hose. Because it is also used as a power inflator, familiarity with the location is greatly enhanced. Because of constant repetitious use as a power inflator, it requires only a short period of time to develop an automatic response or behavior pattern that is crucial in an out-of-air emergency. Because of the mounting design of the A.I.R. 2, the mouthpiece always faces the diver in optimal alignment for immediate use.

Aside from design, the major difference between an octopus and the safe-second/power inflator systems is in the way they're used. As discussed earlier, an octopus is meant to be given to the out-of-air diver, whereas with units like the A.I.R. 2, the out-of-air diver (receiver) is given the primary second-stage and the A.I.R. 2 is used by the assisting diver (donor). Obviously in the case of solo diving, an out-of-air buddy isn't a concern, but primary second-stage failure is. It is for this reason that a Type I EBS is required; the Type II system is necessary if the solo diver encounters an out-of-air situation with their own primary air supply.

In addition to the convenient location of the Scubapro A.I.R. 2, there are a variety of advantages that it offers. As stated by Scubapro, "The problems associated with the accumulation of sand, gravel, and foreign matter inside the back-up regulator have been solved in the design of the A.I.R. 2 in two ways. First: because the A.I.R. 2 is attached to the shorter buoyancy control hose, it is less likely to drag on the bottom. Second: every time air is "dumped" from the buoyancy compensator it is routed around the regulator mechanism and out through the mouthpiece and exhaust valve. This constant flushing action keeps the breathing chamber clear of foreign material and ready for instant use."

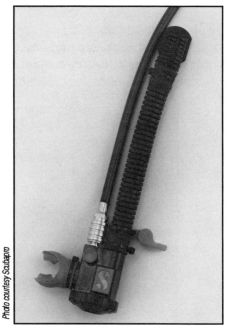

Scubapro **A.I.R. 2**

The A.I.R. 2 has a fiberglass reinforced polyester case, silicone diaphragm, stainless steel springs, and chrome-plated brass regulator mechanism, all of which make the unit extremely durable.

Of all the safe-second/power inflator units described in this text, I have had the most experience with the Scubapro A.I.R. 2. It has always performed well in and out of the water both as a second-stage regulator and power inflator.

Sea Quest **Air Source**

The Air Source from Sea Quest is a comparatively new safe-second/power inflator on the market. Like the others included in this chapter, I have included it because of its track record. Although the Air Source hasn't been around for an extensive period of time, it has already developed an excellent reputation as a reliable and durable Type I EBS.

The Air Source differs from the A.I.R. 2 in many ways, the most obvious of which is in the way the unit is used for oral BCD inflation. With the Scubapro A.I.R. 2, oral inflation is accomplished by using the regulator's mouthpiece. With Sea Quest's Air Source, the diver orally inflates the buoyancy compensator via a specially designed orifice located on the top of the unit. This provides the user with two separate airways, one for oral inflation and an additional one, the regulator mouthpiece, for breathing.

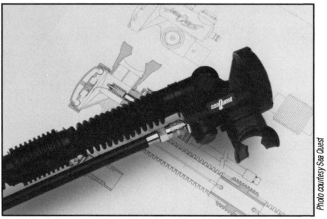

Sea Quest **Air Source**

The Air Source is currently available in two colors - black and day-glo green. I have seen both colors in the water and the green was by and large the most visible of the two. I have also had the opportunity to dive with the unit on a number of occasions and was impressed by it's performance both as a safe-second regulator and power inflator. It is constructed of high impact, corrosion resistant Delrin® with a silicone diaphragm and exhaust valve, and stainless steel demand lever. All other metal parts are chrome-plated or stainless steel, to resist corrosion and provide long life.

Three different configurations of the unit are available: The Air Source with Versavalve Airway, including Trim Grip and LP inflator hose; The Air Source with Trim Grip and LP inflator hose; and The Air Source with LP inflator hose.

Zeagle **Octo +**

Another Type I EBS on the market that has earned an excellent reputation is Zeagle's Octo +. It is again a safe-second/power inflator device that is attached to the inflator hose on the buoyancy compensator.

The Octo + is manufactured by Apeks Marine Equipment Ltd. of England and is exclusively distributed in the United States by Zeagle Systems, Inc.; a company that is well known for its buoyancy compensators that integrate both the BCD and weights into one unit, thus eliminating the need for a weight belt.

Zeagle's Octo + is similar to Sea Quest's Air Source in that it incorporates a separate orifice for oral BCD inflation. Breathing from the regulator is accomplished via the regulator's mouthpiece.

Zeagle **Octo +**

I have used the Octo + myself and also know divers who use it regularly. It has proven to be a most reliable Type I EBS as well as a responsive power inflator. The housing is made of high-impact polymer making it a very durable unit.

Tekna **Second Wind**

The Tekna Second Wind is an altogether different concept in emergency breathing systems due to the fact that instead of being a safe-second/power inflator combination that is melded into one unit, it is a Type I EBS that attaches directly to the base of the Tekna power inflator, thus providing the diver with a completely separate octopus regulator and avoiding the need for an additional low-pressure hose coming from the first stage.

The unique design of the Second Wind has the same important advantage that the three previously discussed systems provide: location. Since it is connected to the base of the power inflator, the diver's familiarity with the location of the EBS will be increased each time the power inflator is utilized.

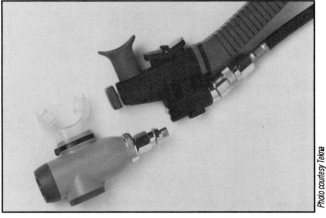

Tekna **Second Wind**

One unfortunate drawback to the Second Wind is that it can only be used with a Tekna power inflator. Hopefully, Tekna will eventually design a similar model that is compatible with other manufacturers' inflators. (I have heard that plans are already on the drawing board for just such a model.) Although I have not had the opportunity to dive with the Second Wind, I have spoken to several divers who have and their response was proof that it is indeed an excellent unit.

Sherwood **Shadow**

The Sherwood Shadow is a Type I EBS that attaches directly to the low-pressure connector on the power inflator.

Sherwood **Shadow**

It too is designed to be used by the assisting diver (donor), while the primary regulator is given to the out-of-air diver (receiver).

The Shadow is constructed of lightweight Lexan® and incorporates a special fulcrum design that helps resist free-flowing during entries and high current situations.

I have dived with the Shadow on numerous occasions and found it to be an excellent Type I EBS that performs quite well.

TYPE II: REDUNDANT AIR SUPPLY

As a solo diver, you may decide not to dive with a Type I EBS (although it is highly recommended), but any solo diving attempted without a Type II EBS would be unadulterated foolishness. Due to the fact that you alone provide your only back-up air supply, to solo without one is not only foolish, but unsafe as well. As stated earlier in the chapter, a Type I system is ideal for primary second-stage malfunction, but does not serve the purpose of an emergency back-up; that's what a Type II system is all about. If you're underwater and all alone, you'd damn well better have an emergency air supply.

I've already eluded to the fact that out-of-air situation can happen to even the most diligent divers. In a readership survey conducted a few years ago by **Discover Diving** magazine (April/May 1987), it was discovered that out of all the divers who responded to the survey, 34% had experienced at least one form of an emergency out-of-air emergency – 31% more than once. In a majority of the incidents a buddy was present, but in nearly 40% of the reported cases the emergency was due to an equipment failure of one form or another. The laws of probability tell us that if enough dives are performed, an emergency of one type or another is bound to occur, and the chances of that emergency involving the diver's air supply are greater than many others. A back-up, redundant Type II emergency breathing system will place the odds in favor of the diver.

In order to select the appropriate back-up system it's important for the diver to examine exactly what type of coverage and redundancy is needed and then decide which Type II system would best fit the situation. The ideal Type II system would allow the diver to extricate him/herself from an out-of-air situation by ascending at a safe, normal rate (60 feet per minute) and avoiding a possible lung overexpansion injury. Another consideration would be stage decompression diving. If a particular back-up system did not allow the diver enough reserve air to make a required stop(s), then it would be considered insufficient. I'll admit that a missed decompression stop is certainly less severe than drowning, but if both can be avoided by diving with the proper equipment, so much the better.

I have treated the various Type II systems in much the same manner that I explained the Type I systems. Each is given a brief description that explains how it is used and for what type of diving it would best apply. Also, in Table 5.1 I have outlined each Type I and II system discussed, its use (fault coverage), emergencies that it won't apply to, and disadvantages.

I would like to again reiterate the fact that solo diving should always be performed with at least some form of a Type II system, and the addition of a Type I EBS should also be considered. Redundancy is an important concept that all divers, particularly solo divers, would be wise to factor into their equipment considerations, and depending on the type of diving conducted, it is crucial to safety that the proper system and level of redundancy be selected in order to insure that the diver's emergency needs are met.

As divers, we have grown accustomed to hearing about various laws (Boyle's, Henry's, Dalton's, etc.), but let's not forget the ubiquitous Murphy and his laws. By realizing that if something can go awry, it will, we can better prepare to avoid a situation that might otherwise cost us dearly. What is it they say about foresight – "An ounce of prevention...".

Submersible Systems, Inc. **Spare Air 3000**

Submersible Systems, Inc. of Huntington Beach, California has been instrumental in developing Type II redundant air systems. With the initial introduction of the Spare Air a few years ago, the sport diving industry (particularly the instructional agencies) has taken a long, hard look at redundancy and back-up air systems.

The newest of the Spare Air units to hit the market is the 3000 series Spare Air model 270, a completely redundant Type II system that contains 2.7 cubic feet of air (3000psi). The unit is reasonably small (see photo below), and weighs only 1.75 pounds out of water and is neutrally buoyant in water. It is considerably different than its predecessor in that it not only contains more air, but is slightly shorter (albeit a larger diameter) with a flip valve instead of a screw-type valve. The Spare Air 3000 is sold with a totally redesigned universal mounting system and an adapter that allows the diver to fill it from their scuba cylinder.

It not only serves as an emergency back-up system for the solo diver, but in the case of a buddy running out of air it allows the assisting diver to be completely detached from the out-of-air diver by virtue of the fact that the unit is simply handed over to the diver in trouble. No hoses or lines of attachment are necessary, thereby making the process considerably more safe than a sharing air ascent via an octopus or safe-second/power inflator. The Spare Air 3000

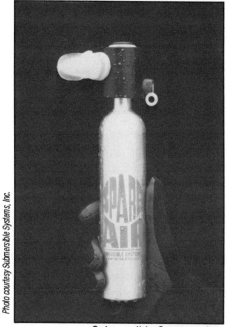

Photo courtesy Submersible Systems, Inc.

Submersible Systems, Inc.
Spare Air 3000

is designed to be carried in a nylon, velcroed holster that can be positioned in a variety of locations on the diver such as along the BCD waist strap or on the cylinder.

I personally dive with a Spare Air and recommend it to my students. I have fortunately not been placed in a position where I needed to use it, but I have simulated many emergency ascents with my students as well as practicing with it solo. On all occasions, the unit has performed efficiently and without incident. Nathan Rosenberg, Chairman and President of Submersible Systems, Inc. stated that, "Our new Spare Air is the product of our emphasis on serving our customers. Each improvement was based on suggestions from divers, instructors, and diving retailers."

The Spare Air 3000 is an excellent choice for sport/recreational diving that doesn't involve overhead environments, deep water (i.e. 80+ feet/24+ meters), or any other type of advanced, specialized situations. Not that it couldn't be included as an additional form of redundancy in such cases, but as a first-line Type II EBS it most likely would not supply the diver with enough emergency air.

Pony Bottle

The preferred Type II emergency breathing system for wreck divers appears to be the pony bottle: a 20 to 40 cubic foot scuba cylinder that has a completely separate set of regulators and gauges (the gauges are often omitted) attached to it. It supplies the diver with an adequate air reserve for all but the most advanced types of diving. For the solo diver it is an excellent choice due to the fact that it has such a large capacity of air.

A pony bottle is usually attached to the primary cylinder via any number of devices, most of which involve some type of harness (such as the Scuba Stuff Pony Packer) to secure the EBS in a position that would allow the diver to easily access the reserve. I've seen divers who concocted various ways to attach the emergency regulator to their buoyancy compensator and in other cases I've seen the back-up regulator dangling freely at their side or behind them (certainly not the best possible scenario). The regulator that is attached to the pony bottle should be treated like an octopus in that it is important to have it secured in a safe, easily accessed location. Additionally, any other hoses that may be attached to the reserve regulator need to be secured so that they don't become entangled or fouled.

For any solo dives that exceed a depth of 80 feet (24m) it is highly recommended that an emergency breathing system with at least the reserve capacity of a pony bottle be utilized. At such depths, a Type II system such as the Spare Air just wouldn't provide the diver with an adequate emergency air supply.

Independent Doubles

For years divers have used a cylinder configuration that is referred to as "twins" or a standard doubles manifold. This is a rig that is composed of two cylinders of the same size connected via a single valve, single regulator seat manifold. Twins provide the diver with double the amount of air than that provided by a single cylinder. I have used twin 80s on many occasions, primarily for deep or wreck dives. The additional amount of air that they supply is certainly beneficial for extended bottom times, but by themselves they do not provide, nor are they designed as, an emergency air supply.

Independent doubles are composed of a similar configuration to twins. The primary difference is that instead of the manifold providing a single valve and single regulator seat, it supplies the diver with dual valves and two regulator seats. This provides the diver with two completely independent systems: one for primary use and one for emergency back-up. By allowing an individual to turn on or off either regulator (independently), it adds an additional margin for safety.

The dual valve manifold was designed by the cave diving community for use in overhead environments and has since been used by other communities of divers as well (deep, wreck, search and salvage, etc.). By supplying two cylinders, each with their own set of regulators and gauges, the level of redundancy achieved is far greater than that of a pony bottle or Spare Air. The disadvantage is that this type of rig is comparatively bulky and cumbersome, requiring a little getting used to. Also, because of the additional weight of the extra cylinder and regulators, it is necessary for the diver to make adjustments in the amount of weight carried on the weight belt or, in the case of an integrated BCD (buoyancy compensator/ballast), to adjust this amount as well.

Sherwood has designed a system that goes one step further than the typical independent doubles rig. It's called the DIN Double (Genesis) Manifold and employs a unique isolation valve that can be used to isolate either cylinder. The system represents a truly independent EBS that allows for maximum redundancy, and due to the fact that it also incorporates DIN connectors, it offers far greater reliability than a standard yoke.

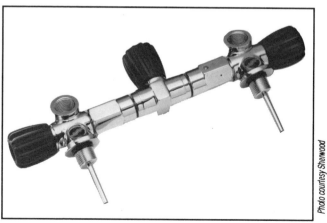

Sherwood **Genesis Manifold**

Table 5.1

Emergency Breathing Systems

Emergency Breathing Systems	Emergencies Covered							Disadvantages
	Out-of-Air Buddy	Out-of-Air Solo Diver	First Stage Failure	Second Stage Failure	Blown O-ring	Ruptured Burst Disc	Shattered Valve	
Type I								
Octopus/Safe **Seconds**	X			X				Can become fouled if not properly secured. Requires additional LP hose.
Scubapro **A.I.R. 2**	X			X				
Sea Quest **Air Source**	X			X				
Zeagle **Octo +**	X			X				
Tekna **Second Wind**	X			X				Currently can only be used with Tekna Power Inflator.
Sherwood **Shadow**	X			X				
Type II								
Submersible Systems **Spare Air 3000**	X	X	X	X	X	X	X	Minimal air supply. Not sufficient for some environments.
Pony Bottles	X	X	X	X	X	X	X	Minimal air supply. Not sufficient for some environments.
Independent Doubles	X	X	X	X	X	X	X	Bulky: size & weight
Sherwood **Genesis Manifold**	X	X	X	X	X	X	X	Bulky: size & weight
Dual Cylinders w/ separate regs & SPG	X	X	X	X	X	X	X	Bulky: size & weight

Solo diving in advanced, specialized environments such as deep wrecks or caves demands maximum air supply redundancy, not only for out-of-air emergencies, but also for other emergencies such as first stage failure, blown O-ring(s), a ruptured burst disc, or a shattered valve. All of these scenarios require a Type II EBS that can be easily accessed and is highly reliable. Independent doubles or Sherwood's Genesis Manifold both offer just such a combination (remember, a Type I EBS should also be standard gear for solo divers).

Dual Cylinders with Separate Regulators and SPG

This type of gear configuration involves two separate, independent scuba cylinders each supplied with their own regulators and SPG. The size of the cylinders is usually the same, but I have seen divers with two different sizes (e.g. one 80 and one 50). Both are attached to the same back pack with each set of regs and gauges located in different positions. The primary set is in whatever position the diver prefers, and the emergency back-up set is usually secured in a BCD pocket or, as I have seen, attached to special clips. I also know divers who secure the emergency regs and SPG to the cylinder via a hodgepodge of velcro and nylon webbing. Whatever the attachment site for the EBS, it's vitally important that they be easy to access and protected from dragging, banging, fouling or various other predicaments that may render them useless.

Obviously, the level of redundancy with this type of set-up is ideal for advanced diving environments where a completely independent emergency breathing system with a comparatively large reserve air supply is required. The primary disadvantage is in the bulk of the extra cylinder and regs, a factor that, as mentioned above, takes a bit of getting used to.

In Chapter 6 we will review various opinions about solo diving from a distinguished selection of individuals. Each opinion is that person's response to a single question: Why Do You Solo Dive?

Chapter 6

Opinions

It is no light matter to make up one's mind about anything, and once made up, it is even harder to abandon the position. When a hypothesis is deeply accepted it becomes a growth which only a kind of surgery can amputate. Thus, beliefs persist long after their factual basis have been removed, and practices based on beliefs are often carried on even when the old beliefs which stimulated them have been forgotten.

John Steinbeck
The Log from the Sea of Cortez

In this chapter we will review the opinions of various individuals from many facets of the sport diving industry. Each opinion author has been asked to respond to a single question - WHY DO YOU SOLO DIVE? For the most part, the opinions have not been edited and are presented here in the same context that they were submitted. Additionally, they are not presented in any particular order or arrangement.

The opinion authors were chosen from a long list of diving professionals and, as the reader can note from the biographical information that appears after each opinion, they were selected for their prominence and experience. For those of my colleagues who doubted that industry leaders such as these would speak out publicly in favor of diving solo, I offer the following pages as proof that there are indeed a wide selection of individuals from across the United States who possess enough fortitude to address the issue in written format. In response to those individuals who, when queried, elected not to go public with their opinions, but rather decided to bury their heads in the sand (*see Chapter 4 for further comments along these lines*), I offer a prayer of hope that they too will one day find the self-esteem to confront reality. To those whose opinions appear within this chapter, I offer a sincere word of thanks for their cooperation and candor.

As a professional diver I frequently practice solo diving as a matter of necessity and convenience. Many underwater photography subjects are best captured on film by one diver who is less obtrusive and can immediately react to an animal's movements without regard for a buddy. I prefer to work this way and the majority of my finest published shots have been obtained while diving alone.

A second situation presents itself when I supervise scuba divers in tropical resort settings. In most cases, the types of divers that request or require the direct supervision of a guide lack the experience and training to be considered a functional buddy to a seasoned professional. Even though I may have other divers with me, I am essentially diving alone since their less experienced status largely renders them ineffective. I can be responsible for their safety, but it is highly unlikely that they can be responsible for mine.

Solo diving is widely practiced. The solo diver must have finely honed diving skills and be acutely aware of his own limitations. Good dive planning, watermanship and self-rescue skills are a necessity. Unless I am fortunate enough to have a dive buddy whose skills, stamina and interests are similar, I prefer to dive solo and not bear the responsibility for another diver's safety. This allows me more personal and professional freedom in the circumstances of the dive and I derive more pleasure from the experience. Both solo diving and buddy diving provide valid choices of dive styles. There are a few skilled divers that I genuinely enjoy sharing my dives with, but those opportunities for shared experiences are rare especially considering that I average over 600 dives annually.

Less experienced divers should stick with the buddy system or dive guide system until seasoned enough to made an informed decision on their ability and personal needs.

I have practiced solo diving for over 20 years and have yet to encounter a situation where a buddy was necessary for me. Conversely, on several occasions when I was counting on support from a buddy diver, that support was sadly lacking. This placed me at risk by relying on the skills and judgement of another diver instead of my own. Diving within one's limitations and strict attention to personal dive situations works best for me.

BRET GILLIAM, President, OCEAN TECH

(20 year industry veteran; over 12,000 dives in career including new world record deep dive on AIR to 452 feet in 1990 while solo; Involved in all phases of dive resort and liveaboard/ship operations.)

I started scuba diving in the late 1950's with my father as my teacher. When the dive industry started talking about requiring a certification card to fill scuba tanks, my father enrolled me in a ten dollar scuba class taught by Jim Stewart of Scripps Institution of Oceanography, but I failed the final written exam. So my father then enrolled me in a twenty-five dollar class at the Diving Locker taught by Chuck Nicklin. Finally, in January 1961, I was a certified diver and Dad had a C-card he could use to fill his tanks. Back in those days the main reason for diving was to kill something – lobster, abalone, fish or whatever. Hunting and buddy diving is very difficult unless there is one hunter and one follower. But at that time everyone was a hunter so diving alone was just the way it was done. I do not mean diving alone was taught, but once you were out of the classroom, the real world was diving alone. So the reason I dive solo now is because that was the way I was brought up in the diving world.

For me, diving alone is not a problem. Through the years I have learned to be self-sufficient. I keep a very close watch on my air supply. I have learned to navigate by natural means so I usually know where I am. I pay very close attention to currents since I am often alone and cannot rely on someone else to bail me out of a situation. Basically, what I am saying is that I am very cognizant of every particular dive situation and have learned to watch out for myself and not to depend on someone else.

LARRY S. COCHRANE, Owner/Operator, Lois Ann Dive Charters, San Diego, California

(Over thirty years sport diving experience; has been involved in many aspects of diving including film making, blue water shark diving, deep diving, cave diving, wreck diving, and many years of experience as a professional divemaster/charter boat captain.)

You're only as alone as you feel.

Many times I dive alone. Most times, I prefer it that way. Selfish? Maybe. Self-sufficient is more like it.

Don't get me wrong. I think buddy diving is absolutely wonderful–with the right person. But it can be a mixed blessing – or an absolute disaster if you're paired with the wrong partner. It's as complex as any topside relationship and it comes with an awesome responsibility. You have someone else's life in your hands.

Some days I just don't want to deal with that. And some days I don't want to hold someone else back because my personal comfort zone has shrunk for one reason or another. Why should I impose my limits on someone else? Or vice-versa? I've been fortunate enough to dive with some of the best people in the ocean, but I find I can become dangerously complacent if I don't get in a little solo time now and then. It's way too easy to believe in the fallacy that your buddy is there to keep you out of trouble. That's your job.

I'm fortunate because my instructor stressed self-sufficiency, self-rescue, and most of all, staying within your own comfort zone. That's why, the first time I lingered too long over a lobster hole and lost my far more experienced buddy, I didn't panic or waste my brief bottom time bouncing back to the surface. Instead I enjoyed being alone with the ocean, as I have so many times since.

CATHIE CUSH, Professional Free-lance Writer/Editor

(Certified as a NAUI Instructor 1987; over 400 logged dives in fresh-and saltwater in many parts of the world including dives on the *Andrea Doria* and the *U.S.S. Monitor*; Managing Editor, **Scuba Times** (1983); Public Relations/Advertising for Beneath the Sea, Princeton Tectonics, Annual DAN Treasure Hunt at Dutch Springs, Underwater World and World of Innerspace; Has also written myriad articles for a host of diving and non-diving publications.)

As a child I played in the ocean long before man built the technology that permitted him to breathe under the water. I felt the surge against my spindly legs. I noted the coolness of the water and the power of the smallest waves against my knees and thighs. I floated, rolled, and ducked, and my face got wet and I swallowed water. I learned to stand firm amidst crashing waves, and I learned to judge their power and their speed. I rode the power and in semi-flight the foaming wave would scarcely touch my belly. In perfect step with my developing skills, I fell beneath the surface, and discovered the bottom of my sea. With eyes wide I probed the sand and when I saw my first fish the sea forever changed.

I grew older, and with a face mask and fins the underwater world opened its windows to my starving curiosity. On my own I ventured out to where the water was well above my head, and I learned to feel myself in the water, to gauge a current and register a wave, to understand the creatures and the gentleness of their ways. I was a free diver and my experience was direct, shot straight into the veins, unadulterated by myth, or false tales, or technology. I saw the real thing, felt my own sensations, discovered the ocean and myself in it at the same time. Everywhere I went I found my own comfort zone. Then came along wetsuits and big spearguns and I ventured into blue fathoms. As far as one could go. I dived the kelp beds and the reefs of coral, and the infinite depths where no kelp or coral could be found. I flew soundlessly in exhilarating flight and heard the sounds of the seas, felt its deep rhythms, and listened to my own rhythms. The vast wilderness of the underwater environment absorbed me into its tissues, whispered its secrets, revealed its hidden places, provided me with food and serenity. The oceans breathed a life into me that I could have never conjured up on my own, and I will forever be in its debt.

I dive alone, and it has always been that way. I may enter the ocean with another, but we soon part and go our own way. His ocean is not my ocean, his comfort zone is not my comfort zone. The secrets I have were given to me because I went alone, and in the silence of myself I could hear them. Such secrets are not, cannot, be given when in the company of others, nor can they be seen or heard without a fearless heart and a quiet mind. When in that state one will recognize home, and there the secrets of the ocean will be whispered and further explorations encouraged.

It has been said that the only exploration of value is of one's self. If that is true, then I have had no better teacher in life than the ocean.

CARLOS EYLES, Author

(35 years of diving experience; world famous free diver; author of **Sea Shadows**, **Diving Free**, **Last of the Blue Water Hunters**, and **Sea Stalking**; Has also written numerous articles for several diving publications and is a frequent contributor to **Discover Diving** magazine.)

I am usually professionally employed in dual roles when diving: underwater model or dive guide/instructor. Both require a high degree of individual responsibility and in many ways are similar to pure solo diving. Modeling frequently puts me and the photographer sufficiently far apart so that in an emergency or out-of-air situation I would be forced to deal with the situation alone. We discuss this in advance and assume that I will deal with the situation accordingly. The photographer is usually deeper than the model to effect high sun angles and uses far less air than the model who is doing repeated "swim-throughs" to get the shot. I also wear a 50 or 65 cubic foot tank for better body proportion, and in swim suit shots no BC is worn. Buoyancy control is governed by precise weighting and breath control. I am usually last to enter the water allowing the photographer to set up so I don't waste air. On the surface we make arrangements to rendezvous. After I enter the water, I navigate to his location. Virtually all of my time is spent alone on these dives.

Typically, as a dive guide I deal with divers who are not really qualified to play a real buddy role for me due to their lack of experience, so again I am essentially solo diving.

Outside of work, I practice solo diving about 50% of the time as a matter of convenience and preference. I have to squeeze my personal diving around my professional duties and this usually means no buddy is available. I've yet to experience a problem and approach solo diving specifically as a venture requiring total self-sufficiency and self-rescue.

LYNN HENDRICKSON, Professional Underwater Model

(Instructor/Dive Guide; Dive Boat Captain for *SEA VENTURES* liveaboard cruises in Bay Islands; professional underwater model.)

I make my living filming marine life. People often ask me, "What's the most dangerous animal you've encountered underwater?" I always try to answer honestly, "Other divers." In two decades of diving, the closest I've come to losing my life came as the result of a mistake made by another diver (who was not even my buddy!). The undeniable truth is that many more divers are killed each year because their buddies got them in trouble than are killed in a decade of dangerous marine life attacks.

New divers tend to depend upon their more experienced buddies for help and guidance. Perhaps that's inevitable. But every diving student should be taught to understand that they are entirely on their own even when within arm's reach of their buddy. And diving instructors should be honest about the statistics for buddy breathing. It kills as often as it saves. That may hold true for the buddy system in general.

I seldom dive alone. My work often requires the cooperative effort of several divers. But I always assume I am entirely alone down there and I don't practice any specific buddy diving techniques.

The buddy system has obvious advantages for new divers. But these new divers are always safety liabilities for their more experienced buddies. If I can't dive with someone whose skills approach my own, I'm safer diving alone.

I think diving alone is less enjoyable than sharing the experience with another diver. But depending on that diver for one's survival can be mutually fatal.

HOWARD HALL, Howard Hall Productions

(Over 20 years diving experience in locations throughout the world; award-winning photographer and underwater cinematographer; author of **Howard Hall's Guide to Successful Underwater Photography** as well as numerous magazine articles; winner of the WILDSCREEN competition for his film *Seasons of the Sea*.)

Even when I dive with a buddy, I'm diving alone. In other words, the people I usually dive with are independent. We keep a loose, roaming eye on one another, rather than a constant watch. However, if I can't find a buddy whose diving habits I know and who knows my habits well, I prefer to be on my own. Diving solo allows me to concentrate on the business at hand, whether that is underwater photography, spearfishing or simply studying the intricate formations of life. In many ways it keeps me more alert to my surroundings, especially my depth, location and air consumption. I know I can only rely on myself if danger arises and that seems to heighten the senses. Even though I enjoy solo diving, I don't consider myself a reckless diver. When I'm alone, I'm more cautious. I think twice before penetrating a wreck or entering the mouth of a cave. I don't dive solo to break any records or impress women. Basically, I do it for the freedom and the exhilaration. But I keep it simple. Like the song says, "Freedom's just another word for nothing left to lose." That's not my kind of freedom, I have plenty to lose when diving solo so I'm careful and judicious because I want to keep diving, with or without a buddy, for a long time.

FRED GARTH, Publisher/Editor, Scuba Times Magazine

(Over twenty years of diving experience; made his first solo dive at age 12 in Lake Lanier, GA; Publisher/Editor **Scuba Times**, an international diving publication with offices located in Florida since 1979.)

I meet a large number of divers in the course of a day's work, the majority of which fall into two categories; those who are newly certified, and those with a great deal of underwater experience. A large percentage of the experienced, more advanced divers actively participate in solo diving. Many of these same divers have chosen one particular facet of diving as their specialty. These specialties often include either photography or hunting, both of which tend to lead one into solo diving or at least buddy separation. Photographers particularly tend to become oblivious to the whereabouts of their buddy (a form of solo diving). As a diving instructor I not only solo dive, but when I enter the water with six students I am in fact diving with six liabilities; a form of diving that is without question more dangerous than diving alone. For me, diving is a means of fun and relaxation. While teaching can often be fun, it is sometimes far from relaxing; that's why when I'm in the water and not teaching, I usually dive alone. Going solo is a refreshing change with no one to look out for except myself. Diving alone keeps me in touch with the reasons why I initially ventured into the sport. Why solo? Why not?

TAB BREWER, Instructor/Manager, Sport Chalet Divers, Escondido, CA

(NAUI Instructor; underwater photographer; world-wide experience in many areas of sport diving including wreck, cave, and deep diving.)

I guess I don't think of diving in terms of solo diving or buddy diving. The way I look at it is, when you're underwater you should be prepared and able to take care of yourself. That means having proper working equipment, planning for redundancy, being versed in emergency procedures and most important, diving within your limits whether it's a 60 foot reef dive or a 250 fsw mixed gas wreck penetration. If you go down depending on someone else to bail you out if you get into trouble, you're already over your head.

That doesn't mean of course that someone else can't help you, or that you shouldn't be prepared to help others, it just means you shouldn't depend on someone for help, because chances are, it won't be there when you need it.

As far as my own diving goes, I frequently dive alone because I enjoy it, it's convenient, and many times, it just fits my objectives better. There are other times I dive with a partner, both for enjoyment or because of a shared objective. However, I think the important thing when you are diving with someone is to be clear about the agreements you have, whether it's sticking together, or following the dive plan, and honoring those agreements.

MICHAEL MENDUNO, Publisher, AquaCorps Journal

(14 years diving experience in many advanced areas such as deep, wreck, cave, mixed gas; PADI Divemaster; Publisher and Senior Editor **AquaCorps: The Journal for Experienced Divers**; frequent contributor to **Discover Diving** magazine and author of several high-tech diving articles.)

I've spent a great deal of time underwater both as a civilian and involved in various military operations. The majority of these dives have been solo. If an individual is considering solo diving they need to be fully aware of the prerequisites: complete self-sufficiency, 100% competence, and proper physical conditioning. Provided these criteria are met, the only dangerous aspect of diving alone is maintaining control of your imagination.

A.J. LaCHANCE, U.S. Navy Seal

(Over six years as a Navy Seal; Open Ocean Insertion Instructor, Jumpmaster, and Master Parachutist (USN); NASE Instructor Trainer/Course Director.)

Let me begin by dispelling some negative connotations which have been attributed to "solo" diving by assuring you that:

1) I do not solo dive because I am a rebel like Madonna, the controversial rock star, intent on shocking and outraging people.

2) I do not harbor a neurotic death wish, nor am I a "Dare Devil", "Hot Dog", or "Danger Junkie". On the contrary, I am probably the most careful, safety-conscious diver I know.

3) I do not solo dive to look "macho", or to make a "I'm just as tough as you are, big guy!" statement. I enjoy being an extremely feminine lady, both in and out of the water.

With all of the above said and done, now I'll tell you why I sometimes do solo dive. First, as a scuba instructor and an underwater photographer and model, circumstances often dictate that I dive without a buddy. Additionally, however, I often spend my leisure time diving in and around shipwrecks in the North Eastern U.S., and have been doing so for almost fifteen years. The North East is a challenging environment which demands of its divers an exceptionally high level of skill, equipment, responsibility, and physical fitness. I can attest to my own qualifications, and I know and respect my own limits. I can't, however, guarantee that even a highly experienced peer will be an asset as a buddy on any given dive. And a buddy who is not an asset can often be a liability!

Let's face it. Whenever we dive, we do somewhat of a high-wire act. Diving means placing ourselves in an environment which is alien to human physiology. We are deceiving ourselves, and probably even diving less cautiously than we should be, if we think that proximity to another individual will miraculously override this risk. And unfortunately, the "buddy system" all too often is nothing more than just that-proximity-two people sharing the same body of water. As a diving EMT and recompression chamber staff member, the victims of diving accidents and fatalities which have come to my attention were always diving with a buddy.

Solo diving in certain situations, therefore, may be as safe or safer than the buddy system. Solo diving, incidentally, is not necessarily synonymous with solitary confinement. Solo diving to me does not constitute jumping into the ocean and suddenly reappearing sixty minutes later. When I solo dive on a North East wreck, I file a very meticulous dive plan, both written and verbal, with a divemaster, indicating the time of my descent, my planned bottom time, my ascent and safety hang time, and exactly where on the wreck I expect to be. I confirm that during my dive, a divemaster or trained rescue diver will be on board watching for my bubbles. Very often, even though I do not have a buddy, I am within view of other divers. I always carry multiple backup air supplies and safety devices.

But the most important factor in solo diving is the mind-set of the diver. Not surprisingly, it is the same ethic for which I strive, as should all instructors, to instill in scuba students-the assumption of acceptable risk, the responsibility to respect the environment and the confidence to trust one's own skills and judgement. If we do our job as scuba instructors, the divers we produce should all be totally self-sufficient divers. They should be, in essence, solo divers!

HILLARY VIDERS, NAUI 1991 International Conference Program Director

(NAUI Instructor, ITC Staff, and Lifetime Member; recipient of 1990 NAUI Award for Outstanding Service; NAUI Executive Liasion for Marine Conservation and Environmental Affairs; Emergency Medical Technician; American Red Cross CPR Instructor; Crew Member of the North American Hyperbaric Chamber; International Model; Ph.d. Comparative Literature; Public Relations Director of Tri-State Dive Retailers Association.)

The term "solo diver" has many connotations in modern day diving. First, I would prefer to use the term "self-sufficient diver" rather than solo diver. To me, solo implies "completely alone." I generally travel alone much of the time rather than with a companion who dives. This means that I often travel with groups of divers or meet divers at resorts with whom I have not dived previously.

Every time I get on a dive boat I am expected to "buddy" with another diver - only someone I only met the night before. What can I expect from this buddy?

Based on the realities of experience, I find that I and many, if not most, divers are technically alone in the ocean even with the time-honored buddy within touching distance. Have you ever asked yourself, "Could my diving buddy really provide the necessary assistance that I might require in a life-threatening situation?" Far too often the objective answer to this question is "No!"

Diver watching has become one of my hobbies that is only rivaled by fish watching. In fact, the modern day vacationing scuba diver is more colorful than most reef fishes. Color aside, the social and behavioral patterns of vacationing scuba divers are even more interesting than their color display. My observations of these scuba divers began shortly after our flight left Miami. Many of my fellow divers are already numbed by alcohol before they arrive in tropical paradise.

The social behavior pattern will vary significantly with each individual, island, and resort. On at least one Caribbean island, marijuana is available from many taxi drivers so that you can take a few drags on the way to the hotel. At most resorts the welcome cocktail party initiates the social calendar for the week. And there are very few things that a vacationing diver likes more than free or cheap booze. In all honesty, the social environment of a tropical diving vacation is probably the worst possible environment on earth for a scuba diver.

Time for diving, but first I have to pick up lead weights at the dive locker. Many of my fellow divers are in line ahead of me. I listen and observe. Give me 20 pounds! I'll take 25! 22! 30! Why are these divers wearing dry suits in the Caribbean? I hear the guide ask,

"What type of suit are you wearing?" Reply, "Purple dive skin!" The rest of my morning is equally as interesting – equipment assembly, dive table interpretation, entries, half inflated BCDs at 80 feet, kicks, broken coral, and the like. Dives over! It's party time! Nothing like a cold beer on the way back to shore.

This is the first day of a long week. I recall one of these first days three years ago. As everyone donned their scuba for entry I suddenly realized that the only other diver on the boat with an alternate air source (i.e. octopus) besides myself (out of 12 divers) was the dive guide. Right, it was 1988 and some of them were novice divers. It would take an entire book for me to relate my adventures, misadventures, and opinions.

So let's get back to the original question, "Why do I solo dive?" Frankly, I would rather be alone underwater than to be with another diver who's judgement, reasoning, coordination, and reaction time is impaired by the after-effects of alcohol (or maybe worse); who might not have been scuba diving for the past 10 or 12 months; who is 10 pounds over-weighted and who is 40 pounds overweight; who doesn't own an alternate air source; who can't put a back pack on a scuba cylinder correctly; who forgot how to use a dive table (or never learned); and who can barely take care of themselves on the boat let alone underwater. I would also rather dive alone than with someone who received their certification through a home study course and a few hours of resort environment instruction.

So, unless I know my diving buddy, know that buddy's physical and emotional condition, and have dived with that buddy before, I dive solo – self-sufficient – even if I can reach out and touch another diver.

LEE H. SOMERS, Ph.D.

(Ph.D. Oceanography; Associate Research Scientist and Lecturer, Dept. of Atmospheric, Oceanic and Space Sciences, The University of Michigan; Assistant Professor, Dept. of Sports Management and Communication, Division of Kinesiology, The University of Michigan; University Diving Safety Coordinator, Dept. of Occupational Safety and Environmental Health, The University of Michigan; AAUS Founding President and Board of Advisors; NAUI Instructor Trainer/Course Director; NAUI Advisory Board; PADI Master Instructor; Cave Diving Instructor; Ice Diving Instructor.)

I solo dive for a variety of reasons. Probably first and foremost, I solo dive during very technical exploration cave dives, (very small passages, extremely silty, etc.) because I am most comfortable exposing only myself to the inherent risk I face. Often times a second diver increases the risk of a safely executed dive (i.e. more silt, getting stuck, air emergency, etc.). Also if the diver is less experienced, than I am the person who receives the increased exposure of risk. In the limited cases I do solo dive, I am simply not willing to assume the responsibility of another diver who is not prepared for the environment I choose to enter. The second primary reason I solo dive is to be alone, to be with myself and the underwater environment I have entered. As a child when I was bad, I was sent to my room. I was always quite amused by my parents action on this one. The irony lies in the fact that even when I was good I would often go to my room alone anyway. I enjoy time with myself. When diving alone (as long as you do it as safely as you can), you are as alone as you can be especially underwater in a cave. Here I explore not only the place but my innermost self. I enjoy facing

fear and anxiety alone. When I do so successfully I feel more alive, more in control of myself and my goals.

WES SKILES, Founder/President, Karst Environmental Services, Inc.

(Over 20 years diving experience with over 3500 dives; Extensive cave and deep diving experience; Member of NACD and NSS-CDS; NSS-CDS Cave Diving Instructor; World-record for cave penetration and a variety of additional record-breaking projects; Founder and President of Karst Environmental Services, Inc.; Underwater photographer/cinematographer whose work has appearred on National Geographic Explorer and Watersports World Programs.)

Growing up exploring the jetties and snorkeling on the reefs off the coast of Fort Lauderdale, Florida, I became a certified diver at the age of 13. My father and I enrolled in the course together. He helped me with the dive tables and I helped him tread through the water. Scuba diving was fun, but at the same time it deposited a large amount of responsibility on my shoulders. Never before was I held accountable for the welfare of another person's life. I was initially taught to be dependent on a buddy; not only for my own personal safety, but for their's as well.

Through many years of studying the ocean, maintaining a commercial diving business, and pursuing the goals of an underwater cinematographer/producer, I have spent hundreds of hours alone underwater. When asked by Robert to submit this opinion, I told him that I would compare solo diving to driving a car:

Out of all the people that drive/dive, many don't belong on the road/in the water. The environment is safe as long as one understands how their automobile/body will handle gradual or sudden changes, if the respective environment should change (as indeed it will).

The equipment being used by the individual in the particular environment (automobile/dive gear) will perform adequately only if it is properly maintained and, in case of an equipment breakdown or malfunction, it is important for the driver/diver to fully understand how to manipulate it to avoid disaster.

Personal judgement, planning, and experience are all important factors for the solo diver to take into consideration. It's my belief that if a person cannot safely and proficiently deal with the above situations, they should dive with an experienced buddy who is aware of their inadequecies. Also, they may wish to pursue further instruction and training to increase their knowledge and experience. Safe diving.

LANCE MILBRAND, Underwater Cinematographer/Producer

(16 years diving experience; Commercial Diver; Underwater Cinematographer/Producer; President, UAU Productions.)

There are many reasons why I like to dive alone. One word that sums it up is SERENITY. I'm responsible for myself and no one else, and no one is responsible for me. Good solo divers make better buddy divers. If they do dive with a buddy, it's because they want to, it's not because they're buddy-dependent.

Solo diving requires that you not only pre-dive your equipment, but have the proper redundant systems as well (two air supplies, two bottom timers, etc.) I dive with a dry suit and a buoyancy compensator with independent inflators (one on each tank). I also wear my mask strap under my hood so that it can't be knocked completely off my face. I always carry a lift-bag (100 lb. minimum) and a line reel with at least 1 1/2 times the depth of the water.

Different environment dictate different equipment considerations and dive planning (i.e. deep, wreck, drift, cave, etc.). Streamlining your equipment is also another important consideration. I attach my lights, line reel, camera equipment, etc. to a harness, and it also keeps them in front of me where I can get to them easily. I also carry two knives; one on my thigh and one on a console. When I first started diving I did a lot of spearfishing (free diving), and this involved diving alone. In 1961 I was introduced to Al Boehm, then President of the Island Divers Club, a group of solo divers who taught me a great deal about diving.

If you stay in diving long enough, you'll encounter almost every situation that can arise when entering an alien environment. In 1977 I had been diving for 17 years (15 1/2 of them teaching). I thought I had encountered all the situations, I hadn't. While diving the wreck of the SS Oregon, I encountered a most frightening experience. I reached the bottom at about 130 feet with visibility around 50 feet. I was at the forward mast and in the process of removing a block and tackle when suddenly, in my peripheral vision, I noticed a diver bearing down on me like a freight train. I knew he needed air. I put my hand on the safe-second on my chest and extended to him. WHAM! He smashed me in the face, grabbing the regulator from my mouth; flooding my mask and hurting my jaw. I instinctively put my second regulator in my mouth and started to clear my mask. I'm OK I thought as I took my first breath. WHAM! He did it again. This time tearing the safe-second from my mouth and completely flooding my mask (luckily I wear the mask strap under my hood, or it would have been gone). I reached out an pushed him back as I grabbed for one of the regulators, partly clearing my mask at the same time. In all this confusion of air bubbles, sand, and silt, I saw my attacker's hand and grabbed for it. I pushed off the bottom, pulling both of us up. I let go of his hand and he was on his own, so was I. I thank God for all my previous experience that kept me from panicking. I was shaken-up by the experience and ascended quite rapidly, clearing my mask as I ascended. I hit the surface first, the other diver popping up four or five seconds later – spitting out his regulator and screaming, "I COULDN'T GET ENOUGH AIR FROM MY REGULATOR!" When I spoke with him later, he admitted that he had been experiencing anxiety attacks for the last couple of weeks.

Solo diving isn't for everyone. It requires discipline and good judgement (as can be seen from the above scenario), even if this means aborting a particular dive.

CAPTAIN STEPHEN W. BIELENDA, Owner/Operator, Research Vessel *WAHOO*, Miller Place, New York

(Over 30 years diving experience; Master Diving Instructor/Course Director, PADI; Instructor Trainer, YMCA; Consultant, U.S. Coast Guard and U.S. Navy, Explosive Ordnance Department; Underwater Search and Recovery Advisor, New York State, Nassau, and Suffolk County Police Departments; Producer, Helicopter Diver Victim Evacuation Program, Eastern Dive Boat Association/U.S.C.G.; Marine Historian; Owner/Operator, R/V Wahoo; Owner, Under Water Services Unlimited; President, Eastern Dive Boat Association; Board of Directors, Center for Underwater Research and Exploration.)

During my 14 years of diving experience I've had the opportunity to dive an assortment of areas from Australia's Great Barrier Reef to the chilly waters of Alaska. As a professional, safety conscious, and experienced diver, I find solo diving to be a privilege; not to be taken for granted.

So why solo dive? Because I'm not forced to depend on or be responsible for a dive partner. This extra freedom allows me to concentrate on just me and my objectives for a particular dive. Only my decisions will determine the success and outcome of the dive. I dive solo under two different situations. One: when I'm the only diver in the water. Two: when there are other divers in the water, but buddy contact is not consistently kept. In both cases, someone is either on the shore or in a boat keeping track of my movement. The majority of my solo diving tends to be in the latter of the two situations, and only then when certain prerequisites are met.

- If I have previously dived the area in a buddy team. If a great deal of time has passed since last diving the location, I normally conduct a comprehensive skin/snorkel dive to refamiliarize myself.

- The location must be relatively shallow (60 feet or less).

As well as the above prerequisites, certain environments and conditions are more conducive to solo diving than others. Good visibility ranks among the most important factors. Additionally, areas with thick kelp canopies or potentially dangerous marine animals pose a threat to solo divers.

Spearfishing and underwater photography are two activities that I prefer to do solo. They both require that element of surprise in capturing the subject on film or the end of a spear.

Solo diving is not for everyone. Years of training and diving may not make you comfortable diving alone. That's fine, after years of driving a car I wouldn't feel comfortable driving to New York alone! For whatever reason(s) that you decide to solo dive, remember a few key points: There won't be anyone there to untangle you from the kelp, grab your weightbelt that came unbuckled on the reef, pick you up when the surf knocks you down, carry your overweighted game bag back to the boat, or let you share air when your tank runs low. In other words, extreme caution and common sense must always be exercised when diving solo!

DARREN WEBB, NAUI Instructor Trainer/Assistant Diving Safety Officer, San Diego State University

(14 years diving experience; NAUI Instructor Trainer/Assistant DSO, SDSU; Marine Research Diver with extensive deep diving experience from Alaska to Australia.)

Why do I dive solo? Why doesn't everybody? I believe you really don't belong in the ocean if you cannot handle yourself when the situation becomes difficult. It was early on that I decided "buddy diving" was for the birds.

Now, don't get me wrong, I enjoy going in the water and diving with others, but through experiences very early in my diving career, I learned that the only person I could, and should, depend on was myself.

On my third ocean dive, which was in the North Atlantic, I dove the stern half of the tanker Stolt Dagali. It had just met its fate in the fall of 1964. Being a novice diver, I was buddied with two more experienced divers – or so I thought. Both were psychiatrists, older, and supposedly wiser.

On our first dive, the three of us swam around the exterior of the intact stern of the tanker. I even retrieved a brass cage lamo from the mast, just by unscrewing it. While ascending with one of these fellows, we spied an opening into the hull. During our surface interval, we planned a dive to penetrate – the unknown!

For the second dive, only two of us went down. The third man decided not to make the dive. Executing our prearranged plan, the other man and I entered the galley and began looking around. After a while, I looked up and found myself alone with an armload of stainless steel bowls and dishes that had spilled out of the galley. There was a huge hole to the deep, dark, depths right beside me. Where had my buddy gone?

In those days, of course, we had J-valves and no pressure gauges. I had been down for a while and figured I must be getting near the end of my air. Besides, I figured I couldn't carry any more – BC's didn't exist then either and I was very heavy carrying all my loot (no goodie bag either). I made my way down the entire length of the companionway and tried to swim up, with great effort, to the doorway we had entered. There was my buddy, two-hose regulator and all, giving me the out-of-air signal. He zoomed to the surface 60 feet above and left me with my flat, old-style horse collar struggling along. Upon reaching the surface, I heard him yell for help. Being the well-trained lifeguard, Water Safety Instructor person, etc., I dropped my goodies and did an arm assist, towing the dude back to our charter boat - BooHoo for my loot.

Come to think of it, I had buddied with this same person the week before. We went down the anchor line and visibility was so limited I couldn't find him after several minutes. We were in 45 feet of water. I had been taught that if you lose your buddy – come up, regroup, and continue from there. Well, he never came up and I did. The divemaster insisted I get back on the boat, aborting my first dive. I was a poor college dropout and to scrape together enough money for the charter fare had been no insignificant feat. To have to sit onboard while my "buddy" enjoyed his dive led me to the conclusion that buddy diving wasn't all it was cracked up to be.

Now, as an instructor I feel as if I have a double burden. In Northeast conditions, when we at Dudas' Diving Duds take people on their certification dives, we only take a buddy pair and we advocate their watching out for each other. Again, I'm solo diving – keeping an eye on two novices.

Solo diving doesn't necessarily mean going out all alone, with no surface support personnel. It means the buddy with whom I dive should be just as confidant and competent a diver as I am. We hunt lobsters, flounder, and artifacts during the same dive – not necessarily with one diver being the bag person. We don't enact the fairness act of "share and share alike" either. Possession is the diver's delight. Who in this industry doesn't have an ego?

I certainly can't catch lobsters going down the same row of ribs, or stab the same flounder, or carefully penetrate a silt-covered lower deck passageway with a buddy. If you are digging in an area for an artifact with a scooter, it gets very murky. Your buddy doesn't want to be there either. But, occasionally, I am in need of my buddy's muscle power. I'll find an object too heavy for me to move. For instance, there was a solid brass binnacle left behind on a wreck sunk off Atlantic City several years ago as an artificial reef. I was unable to budge it myself, but together, Charlie Dulin and I were able to retrieve it – all 300 pounds of it – in October of 1990.

I like to try to document on film or underwater video what I have seen. Sometimes, when solo diving, you must become your own subject. With video, this is easy; but getting into your own 15mm Nikonos shots is a bit more difficult. Mike DeCamp did it 20 years ago. He C-clamped his Nikonos I to an object and then got in front of his lens, next to a ship's wheel. Incidentally, upon finishing his picture, he gave a tug to his C-clamp and up came a sextant that it was attached to.

I get very tired of trying to compose tube sponge pictures, close-up pictures, and silhouette shots when everyone else is in such a hurry to get down the reef. Where are my subjects? I still shoot with a manual camera system and try to bracket each set-up shot. Nobody likes to dive with me – I go very slowly – and I stay in the water at least one hour, usually one and a half, assuming there are shallows to play in. Many get bored waiting on the boat for me.

I have put in a lot more hours in northern waters in a dry suit, double tanks, and redundant life-support systems than I have in warm waters. But in warm water diving, I'm just as comfortable going night diving alone. My camera is my buddy. Buddies become models or subjects and I find it difficult to convince people to just hang around to pose for my camera – for the two cameras-worth of film I shoot each dive.

If I'm going to dive a deep wreck, I want somebody to check up on me once in a while. I like to share my experience with others, but often I'll get in the water and to the anchor line first. Most of the time waiting for my partner, so we descend at the same time. On the bottom we communicate where we will go and specific rendezvous points, checking on each other from time to time. It's important to really know the other person's dive plan.

I can scare myself sometimes. We all wear upline equipment so we can attach anywhere on the wreck and safely make an ascent, do a safety hang, and the folks on the boat can see that you are OK by seeing that your lift bag stays in place on the surface.

Last summer I swam the entire perimeter of the wreck of the Tolten at 95 feet, in my alloted 25 minutes. The mate had thrown the anchor out of the wreck so there was no anchor line to ascend. I removed my upline reel and proceeded to do all the right things, but halfway up through this procedure my sisal line broke, taking my lift bag with it. Instant panic! What was I going to do? I had to hang. On the wreck I saw another diver's line already in place. It was still extending upward. I hastily swam back and went up this line. It *had just been abandoned and was just beginning to sink to the bottom. After hanging about 10 minutes, my bag and 40 feet of line came floating by. What luck.*

I dive because, in the water, I cannot think of all the other stresses life has brought along. I am totally engulfed in the "now" part of my life when I am underwater.

People ask how I can advocate solo diving when my husband died while diving solo. I suppose it is because I don't believe it was solo diving that killed him. I have never known a better, more competent diver than my late husband, John. Perhaps that is what led to his death. Being very confident in himself and having been diving for so long, he took things for granted. He made a number of relatively small mistakes. He was probably wearing too much weight. He probably should have started up sooner. His primary and back-up regulators might have frozen. He was unaware that his bottom timer was flooded. He was judging his available bottom time on time alone and not tank pressure. Any of these problems, by itself, would not have posed an insurmountable problem to a diver with John's experience and skill. But taken together, they took his life.

Rather than relying on buddy diving, I believe we should stress paying attention to detail. Making sure our equipment is working. Staying aware of our situation. In short, being our own best dive buddy.

EVELYN BARTRAM DUDAS, Dudas' Diving Duds

(27 years diving experience; Instructor; extensive deep and wreck diving experience; first woman to dive the Andrea Doria; recognized as one of the premier divers on the East Coast of the United States; Owner, Dudas' Diving Duds, West Chester, Pennsylvannia; has been profiled in numerous national publications and appears in the DEMA/Jack Mckenney video Scuba America.)

The reason that I dive alone is because, for me, it's more fun. One of the reasons for this is because I see more marine life and I'm able to get completely into my dive. I'm not sure that I'm a very good buddy anyway. Most of my dives involve photography and I'm usually very wrapped-up in marine life. My time in the ocean is so hard to get and once I'm there I just want to enjoy it for all it's worth; I think solo diving allows me to do just that.

As an underwater photographer, I find it annoying to have to be a good buddy. Now, this doesn't mean that I would recommend solo diving to every sport diver. I think there's a psychological dependance on a buddy when you're new to the sport. The ocean is a tough environment and can at times be uncomfortable. To the new sport diver, a buddy can provide a degree of comfort. But I'm not in this just as a sport diver. I've been involved in diving for years and after a while I've become pretty comfortable in the water. Therefore, the more quiet I can be, the less movement around me, and the more natural the environment, the more marine life I can observe and photograph. I also feel that diving alone allows me to get more in touch with the environment.

I'm convinced that once you reach a certain level of competency and once you possess a certain expertise in the ocean environment, diving by yourself is probably a safer way to dive. It's certainly safer than diving with someone you've never dived with before, especially if you're going into the water with a particular objective in mind such as photography. One of the aspects that I like about diving is that its done in a natural environment and you're responsible for everything that you do; the more of that decision making process that I'm involved in, the more easier it is for me to get keyed in to my surroundings.

There's no question in my mind that people can dive alone, and do so very safely. Again, I don't believe that newly certified divers should solo dive, but as a wildlife photographer, solo diving is the best way for me to capture the images that I'm looking for.

MARTY SNYDERMAN, Wildlife Photographer/Cinematographer

(Over 20 years diving experience in myriad environments and locations; PADI and NASDS Instructor; assignment photographer/cinematographer whose work has been utilized by **National Geographic, Oceans, Natural History, Ocean Realm, Underwater USA, Scuba Times**, the Monterey Bay Aquarium, Sea World, and numerous other publications and organizations; Advanced Underwater Photography columnist for **Discover Diving**; author of **California Marine Life** (1988); his film work has been utilized by the National Geographic Society, British Broadcasting Corporation, NOVA, HBO, and numerous other networks and production companies; consultant for See & Sea Travel, Aggressor Fleet, and Nikon, Inc.)

Diving makes demands, certainly, but the rewards it can offer are without measure. To be trained as a diver is to first become comfortable in the environment. Self-assurance leads to that comfort level and the amount of training builds confidence. Experience is also a form of training. There is an incredible amount of experience that can be attained from diving solo.

Like hiking alone in a quiet forest, there is a degree of pleasant solitude while diving alone. The rewards of such solitude are unexplainable to those that have never been there. When I began diving in the 60's, I found this fascinating world and I wanted to share it with others. I became a diving instructor. As a diving instructor, I had to enforce buddy diving techniques, yet instill an overall attitude of self-sufficiency. I soon discovered that while training divers in the open water I was virtually without a buddy. As my diving experience matured, I realized solo diving was part of the experience — part of being comfortable with this environment.

When I was trained as a pilot, the entire emphasis of my training was toward my first solo flight. I was taught to plan flights, to recognize potentially dangerous situations, to react to emergencies, and to know emergency procedures. I was trained to make decisions without my instructor by my side. I was taught to fly solo. Flying and diving have many similarities, and as a diving instructor I taught my students to make these same decisions, but in a different environment.

I like to dive solo. As a professional underwater photographer, it allows me to capture images that I couldn't get close to with an impatient buddy. As a person, it allows me to enjoy the experience that I seek. As a publisher, it allows me to divert my attention away from the phone… at least temporarily…

KEN LOYST, Publisher/Editor, Discover Diving Magazine

(23 years diving experience; Publisher/Editor, **Discover Diving** magazine; author of **Dive Computers: A Consumers Guide to History, Theory and Performance** (1991) and co-author of **Diving with Dive Computers** (1989); NAUI Instructor since 1972; Instructor Trainer since 1976; professional underwater photographer; and private pilot.)

Glossary

This glossary includes diving and diving-related terms as well as terms that may be encountered by divers from areas such as physiology, medicine, marine biology, and oceanography.

A

AAUS
American Academy of Underwater Sciences

ABSOLUTE PRESSURE
Also referred to as "atmospheres absolute", absolute pressure is a measure of the pressure exerted on an object from all sources; includes water pressure (See HYDROSTATIC PRESSURE), and atmospheric pressure.

AERODONTALGIA
Pain in the teeth resulting from a reduction in atmospheric pressure. Also referred to as tooth squeeze.

AEROTITIS
Middle ear squeeze.

AIR CONSUMPTION RATE
See SURFACE AIR CONSUMPTION RATE (SAC RATE)

AIR EMBOLISM
See ARTERIAL GAS EMBOLISM (AGE)

ALVEOLI
Plural of alveolus. It is the alveoli that rupture when a lung overexpansion injury occurs. (See ALVEOLUS)

ALVEOLUS
Small air cells in the lungs.

ALVEOLAR EXCHANGE
The exchange of oxygen for carbon dioxide; occurs in the alveoli.

AMBIENT PRESSURE
The sum of air and water pressure at depth expressed in terms of absolute pressure.

ANOXIA
Deficiency of oxygen.

APHOTIC ZONE
The portion of the ocean where an absence of sunlight prohibits plant growth.

APNEA
The cessation of breathing for short intervals of time.

ARCHIMEDES PRINCIPLE
"Any object wholly or partially immersed in a liquid will be buoyed up by a force equal to the amount of liquid displaced."

ARTERIAL GAS EMBOLISM (AGE)
A lung overexpansion injury that involves air bubbles escaping from the lungs into the pulmonary capillary bed. The bubbles can then travel to the heart and eventually follow the circulatory route to the brain. In severe cases AGE can be fatal. Treatment is immediate recompression in a hyperbaric chamber. Also known as an air embolism.

ARTIFICIAL RESPIRATION
A process by which breathing is restored in a person whose respiration has ceased by alternately increasing and decreasing chest volume while maintaining open airways in nose and mouth passages. Mouth-to-mouth resuscitation is the preferred form of artificial respiration.

ATMOSPHERIC PRESSURE or ATMOSPHERE
A measure of the weight of the atmosphere at sea level, approximately 14.7 psi.

B

BAILOUT BOTTLE
See PONY BOTTLE

BAROTRAUMA
Any pressure-related injury.

BCD
Buoyancy Compensator Device

BENDS
See DECOMPRESSION SICKNESS

BENTHIC
A term pertaining to the sea bottom and the organisms that live there.

BEZEL

A movable ring on a compass or watch that allows for the placing of index marks.

BIOLUMINESCENCE

The production of visible light by living organisms. A phenomenon often encountered by divers while night diving.

BOTTOM TIME

The interval from the start of the dive's descent until the diver's head breaks the surface following ascent. Also calculated from the start of the dive's descent until the beginning of the safety stop. (Some divers do not calculate the safety stop into their total bottom time.)

BOYLE'S LAW

"If the temperature is held constant, the volume of a gas will be inversely proportional to the pressure sustained by it. The density will be directly proportional to it." Boyle's Law explains why a gas will be compressed upon descent and will expand upon ascent. It also explains why a diver uses more air at a greater depth.

BRADYCARDIA

Slowness of the heart beat.

BREAKERS

The water formation or disturbance created when waves crest against a reef, ledge, shore.

BREAKWATER

An offshore structure erected to diminish the force of waves.

BREEZE, STRONG

Wind ranging from 22 to 27 knots per hour.

BUDDY BREATHING

An emergency out-of-air procedure where two divers share one second stage regulator while ascending.

BUOYANCY

The upward pressure exerted by the fluid in which an object is immersed.
(See ARCHIMEDES PRINCIPLE) Diving texts commonly, albeit incorrectly, refer to three types of buoyancy: positive, neutral, and negative. (See Chapter 4)

C

CALM

Atmospheric condition with winds of less than one knot per hour.

CARBON DIOXIDE BUILDUP

See HYPERCAPNIA

CARBON MONOXIDE TOXICITY

A condition that results from breathing air that is contaminated with carbon monoxide.

CARDIO-PULMONARY RESUSCITATION (CPR)

A process utilizing the combination of external heart massage and mouth-to-mouth respiration to artificially maintain the heartbeat and respiration of a victim. All divers should be certified in CPR.

CEILING

A minimum depth to which a diver may ascend without risk of decompression sickness.

CHAMBER

See RECOMPRESSION CHAMBER

CHARLES' LAW

"If the pressure of a gas is kept constant, the volume of the gas will vary directly with the absolute temperature." The importance of Charles' Law for scuba divers is in the fact that a filled scuba cylinder will increase in pressure 5 psi for every degree of Fahrenheit increase. Conversely, the same cylinder will decrease in pressure 5 psi for every degree of Fahrenheit decrease. This explains why the pressure of a cylinder increases if it is left in the heat (e.g. trunk of a car on a hot, sunny day), and will decrease in pressure when exposed to room temperature after a "hot" fill.

CIGUATERA

A poisoning that results from eating certain fish which contain a poison (ciguatoxin). May be fatal in extreme cases.

COASTAL CURRENTS

The movement of water parallel to the shoreline.

CO$_2$ DETONATOR

A mechanical device that allows a BCD or liftbag to be filled quickly with carbon dioxide thus providing rapid floatation.

CREST

The maximum height of a wave.

CYANOSIS

A bluish discoloration of the skin that results from an oxygen deficiency in the blood.

D

DALTON'S LAW

"The partial pressure of a given quantity of gas is the pressure it would exert if it alone occupied the same volume. Additionally, the total pressure of a mixture of gases is the sum of the partial pressures of the components of the mixture." Dalton's Law explains why gases are always present at a certain percentage of the total pressure exerted.

DIVERS ALERT NETWORK (DAN)

A national not-for-profit diving safety organization based at Duke University Medical Center, Durham, NC 27710 (919) 684-2948. DAN provides medical consultations to injured divers, collects and analyzes diving accident statistics, sponsors educational programs, and offers diving accident insurance. The 24-hour Medical Emergency Hotline is (919) 684-8111.

DECOMPRESSION LINE

A line used as a point of reference and loose attachment for divers who are decompressing.

DECOMPRESSION MANAGEMENT TOOLS
Tables, wheels, dive computers, and various decompression software used to manage decompression exposures.

DECOMPRESSION REEL
A diver-carried reel with typically 300 or more feet of line, and a small LIFTBAG that can be tied off to a wreck or weighted and hung from the liftbag in the event of missing the DECOMPRESSION LINE. A standard piece of gear among many wreck/deep divers.

DECOMPRESSION SICKNESS (DCS)
A malady caused by nitrogen bubbles forming in various parts of the body when a diver ascends too quickly and/or exceeds their ceiling. Treatment is carried out in a recompression chamber and depending on the severity of the "hit", may be quite extensive. Also known as the bends and Caisson disease.

DEHYDRATION
A loss of bodily fluids. In divers this can be brought about by diving with a hangover, consuming caffeinated beverages prior to diving, overexertion, or diving when ill.

DIAPHRAGM
1) The membrane separating the abdomen from the thoracic cavity. 2) The flexible material in a regulator separating the regulator's chamber from the water.

DPV
Diver Propulsion Vehicle. Also known as underwater scooters.

DYSPNEA
Difficulty breathing that results from increased depth.

E

EBB CURRENT
An outgoing tidal current that results in lowering the water level.

EMERGENCY SWIMMING ASCENT (ESA)
An independent, emergency ascent made upon depletion of the diver's air supply. Also referred to as an emergency out of air ascent or swimming ascent.

EQUALIZE
To make the pressure the same on both sides of a membrane. Divers equalize their ears and sinuses by swallowing, or pinching the nose and blowing (Valsalva technique).

ESTUARY
The mouth of a river in which the river's current meets the sea's tide.

EUSTACHIAN TUBE
The tube that connects the middle ear with the throat, allowing a diver to clear his/her ears.

F

FATHOM

A nautical unit of measurement equivalent to six feet.

FETCH

"Length of fetch" is the extent of water over which a wind blows and develops waves. The greater the distance, the greater the possibility of large waves developing.

FLOOD TIDE

The incoming tide at its greatest height.

FRINGING REEF

A large coral reef formation which closely borders the shoreline.

G

GALE, STRONG

A wind ranging from 41 to 47 knots per hour.

GAUGE PRESSURE

The pressure that is indicated by a submersible pressure gauge (SPG) which is the pressure relative to ambient pressure.

GUST

A sudden, brief outburst of wind.

H

HEAT EXHAUSTION

A condition resulting from overheating that is characterized by a pale, clammy appearance and weakness.

HEAT STROKE

A condition resulting from direct exposure to high temperatures or the sun. It is characterized by dry skin, weakness, dizziness, nausea, strong, rapid pulse, later becoming weak. Unconsciousness usually follows. Heat stroke is considered more severe than heat exhaustion.

HEMORRHAGE

An abnormal discharge of blood, either internal or external; venous, arterial, or capillary from blood vessels into tissues, into or from the body.

HENRY'S LAW

"If the temperature is held constant, the solubility of any gas in a liquid is directly proportional to the pressure the gas exerts on the liquid." This tells us that a liquid can absorb gas, and the more pressure placed on the liquid, the more of the gas it will absorb. When the pressure on the liquid is released, the liquid becomes supersaturated with the gas and gives it off in the form of bubbles. This is important to divers because the deeper one dives, the more pressure exerted on the diver. Because of the increased pressure, the diver's body will absorb more nitrogen. If the level of nitrogen reaches or surpasses a certain point, the diver will have to make a mandatory decompression stop(s) to allow some of the nitrogen to be outgassed. If the stops are not made and the diver surfaces directly, he/she risks suffering a case of decompression sickness.

HIGH WATER
The maximum height reached by a rising tide.

HOLDFAST
A structure which attaches seaweeds to the bottom or to other substrates.

HOOKAH
An underwater breathing system that utilizes a surface air compressor to supply air to one or more divers.

HURRICANE
An intense storm that originates over open water with counterclockwise winds from 75 to 100 mph. The storm can travel up to 60 or more mph.

HYDROSTATIC PRESSURE
The pressure exerted underwater by the surrounding water column.

HYDROSTATIC TEST (HYDRO)
Test required every five years on scuba cylinders. The test involves pressurizing the cylinder to 5/3 of its working pressure with water used as the medium to provide pressure. Cylinders that fail hydro may not be used for scuba diving.

HYPERBARIC CHAMBER
See RECOMPRESSION CHAMBER

HYPERCAPNIA
An undue amount of CO_2 in the blood. A condition caused in diving by improper breathing patterns.

HYPERVENTILATION
The process of rapidly inhaling and exhaling to purge the body of carbon dioxide, thus decreasing the natural urge to breathe. Hyperventilation is a potentially dangerous practice and can lead to shallow water blackout, unconsciousness, and drowning.

HYPOTHERMIA
A condition in which the deep tissue or core temperature of the body falls below the normal physiological range, approximately 97°F (36°C) and is the temperature at which malfunctions in normal physiology occur. If the core temperature continues to drop, serious consequences could develop.

HYPOXIA
Failure of the tissues to receive sufficient oxygen.

I

INDEX MARKS

The points on the bezel of a compass that provide a place to aim the north-seeking needle in order to stay on a particular course.

INERT GAS NARCOSIS

The intoxicating effect experienced by divers who descend to extreme depths. Nitrogen narcosis, a common form of inert gas narcosis, can be incurred at depths as shallow as 100 feet (30m), and possibly even shallower by individuals who are more susceptible.

INTERNAL VISUAL INSPECTION

Also known as the Tank Inspection Program and the Visual Inspection Program, it is a procedure wherein the interior of the scuba cylinder is inspected for rust, corrosion, pitting, moisture, or any other problem. Most dive stores will not fill a cylinder that does not show evidence of having been tested annually.

INTERTIDAL ZONE

The region of the shoreline defined by the marks of the low and high tide. Also known as the littoral zone.

J

JON LINE

A three to six foot line with a hand loop(s) that can be clipped around a DECOMPRESSION LINE. Named after its inventor, Jon Hulbert, a jon line serves as a dampening device for the up and down motion of the decompression line in rough seas. Also used for DPV tows.

"J" VALVE

Divers' slang referring to a reserve valve on a scuba cylinder.

K

KELP

A group of larger brown seaweeds.

KNOT

A nautical unit of speed equal to one nautical mile or about 1.15 statute miles per hour.

L

LEE

The side of a ship, vessel, island, etc. that is farthest from the point from which the wind is blowing.

LEEWARD TIDE
Tide flowing in the same direction as the wind.

LIFELINE
A floating line trailed from a boat to provide divers something to hold onto. Also referred to as a TAG LINE.

LIFTBAG
A bag-like device that is inflated with air and used to lift various objects from the bottom. Many models are designed with an OVERPRESSURE RELIEF VALVE to allow excess air to escape thus preventing damage to the liftbag.

LIGHT BREEZE
A wind of 4 to 6 knots per hour.

LINE OF SIGHT
See LUBBER LINE

LIVE BOAT DIVING
A type of diving that utilizes a manned, unanchored boat.

LONGSHORE CURRENT
Currents that run parallel to and near the shoreline.

LUBBER LINE
1) The reference line on a compass. 2) The imagined straight line that indicates direction of travel.

LUNG OVEREXPANSION INJURY
An injury to the lung tissues caused by a diver ascending too quickly or holding their breath.

M

MAL DE MER
Seasickness (French)

MAXIMUM DIVE TIME (MDT)
The length of time that may be spent at a given depth without being required to make a mandatory decompression stop. Also referred to as NO-STOP LIMITS and NO-DECOMPRESSION LIMITS.

MEDIASTINAL EMPHYSEMA
A lung overexpansion injury that involves air bubbles escaping from the lungs into the chest area near the heart (mediastinum). Results from ascending too rapidly and/or holding one's breath.

MODERATE BREEZE
A wind of 11 to 16 knots per hour.

MULTI-LEVEL DIVE
A type of dive that involves progressively shallower depths. (Also see SQUARE PROFILE DIVE)

N

NSS-CDS
National Speleological Society, Cave Diving Section

NEAP TIDES
A set of moderate tides which recur every two weeks and alternate with spring tides.

NEKTON
Large, actively swimming marine animals (e.g. dolphins, sharks, marlin, etc.).

NITROGEN
A gas that makes up approximately 78% of the air we breathe; responsible for DECOMPRESSION SICKNESS and NITROGEN NARCOSIS.

NITROGEN NARCOSIS
Loss of judgement and motor skills caused by the narcotic effect of breathing the nitrogen component of air at elevated partial pressures (i.e. depth). Condition alleviated upon ascent. Also known as "rapture of the deep."

NMFS
National Marine Fisheries Service

NOAA
National Oceanic and Atmospheric Administration

NO-DECOMPRESSION LIMITS
See MAXIMUM DIVE TIME

NO-STOP LIMITS
See MAXIMUM DIVE TIME

O

OCEAN CURRENT
The general direction in which waters flow in the ocean; clockwise in the Northern Hemisphere and counterclockwise in the Southern Hemisphere.

OCTOPUS
A Type I Emergency Breathing System that is essentially an extra second stage for use if a buddy runs out-of-air. Also known as a SAFE SECOND STAGE or bipus regulator.

OVERPRESSURE RELIEF VALVE
A device built into buoyancy compensators and LIFTBAGS that allows the escape of expanding air without causing damage to the unit.

OXYGEN
A colorless, tasteless, odorless gas that accounts for approximately 21% of the air we breathe. If deprived of oxygen (a condition known as ANOXIA) the body will cease to function. Too much oxygen (HYPOXIA) results in oxygen poisoning.

P

PARTIAL PRESSURE
The pressure exerted by each gas in a mixture of gases.

PELAGIC
A term pertaining to the waters of the ocean and the organisms that inhabit the water column.

PERIOD
The time required for two successive ocean waves to pass a certain point.

PHYSIOLOGY
The study of the body's actions and reactions. Diving physiology is primarily concerned with the effects of water pressure on the diver.

PHYTOPLANKTON
Microscopic plant members of the PLANKTON.

PLANKTON
Free-floating, usually minute organisms of the sea. (See PHYTOPLANKTON and ZOOPLANKTON)

PNEUMOTHORAX
A lung overexpansion injury that involves air bubbles escaping into the chest area and causing lung collapse. Results from ascending too rapidly and/or holding one's breath.

PONY BOTTLE
A small scuba cylinder; usually 40 cu ft or less. Commonly used as an EMERGENCY BREATHING SYSTEM (Type II). Also known as a BAILOUT BOTTLE.

PRESSURE RELIEF DISC
A safety device built into cylinder valves that prevents internal pressure from reaching dangerous levels. The device must be completely replaced if the disc is ruptured. Also referred to as a burst disc or overpressure relief disc.

PSIA
Pounds per square inch absolute.

PSIG
Pounds per square inch gauge. (See GAUGE PRESSURE)

R

"RAPTURE OF THE DEEP"
Nitrogen narcosis

RECOMPRESSION
The accepted treatment for DECOMPRESSION SICKNESS AND LUNG OVEREXPANSION INJURY. Treatment consists of placing the afflicted diver in a RECOMPRESSION CHAMBER and gradually increasing the pressure as per specific guidelines.

RECOMPRESSION CHAMBER
A usually cylindrical, steel chamber that is used for the treatment of DCS and LUNG OVEREXPANSION INJURY. Also referred to as a HYPERBARIC CHAMBER or CHAMBER.

REPETITIVE DIVE
Any dive that is made within 24 hours of a previous dive.

RESIDUAL NITROGEN
The residual amount of nitrogen left in the body as a result of a previous dive.

RESIDUAL NITROGEN TIME (RNT)
Residual nitrogen expressed in terms of time already spent at depth.

RESIDUAL VOLUME
The quantity of air remaining in the lungs after a forceful exhalation.

RIP CURRENT
A strong, narrow current rushing outward from the shore that results from water being pushed up on the beach by waves moving back out to sea.

RSTC
Recreational Scuba Training Council

RULE OF THIRDS
A rule used primarily by cave and wreck divers that basically states that after having consumed 1/3 of your air supply you should begin your exit from the cave/wreck. The remaining 2/3 air left is used for the exit and ascent.

S

SAFETY OUTGASSING ASCENT PROCEDURE (S.O.A.P.)
A procedure that entails making a safety stop at 15-30 feet (4.5-9.1m) for 3-5 minutes at the end of every dive.

SAND BAR
Sand formation caused by wave or current action.

SCUBA
Self-Contained Underwater Breathing Apparatus

SEMIDIURNAL TIDES
Tidal patterns with two low and two high tides each lunar day.

SHARING AIR ASCENT
An emergency out-of-air procedure where one diver supplies an OCTOPUS for an out-of-air diver. The two divers then ascend while holding onto each other.

SHALLOW WATER BLACKOUT
Underwater unconsciousness caused by excessive HYPERVENTILATION.

SHOAL
A shallow area in a body of water caused by a bank or bar.

SINUS SQUEEZE
Pain and/or tissue damage that is the result of not equalizing properly.

SKIP BREATHING
The dangerous practice of taking a breath and holding it for as long as possible before taking another. It is a practice that saves little if any air and can lead to a LUNG OVEREXPANSION INJURY or other pressure-related injuries.

SLACK TIDE
A point at which TIDAL CURRENTS cease or slacken prior to the change in tidal direction (low to high or high to low).

SLURP GUN
A cylindrical device equipped with a plunger and used underwater to collect small animals.

SMALL CRAFT WARNINGS
Warnings put into effect when winds sustain velocities in excess of 18 knots; small craft are advised to stay in port during such periods.

SPG
Submersible Pressure Gauge

SPRING TIDES
Extremely high and low tides which alternate with neap tides and recur every two weeks.

SQUALL
A short, intense gust of wind that occurs with rain or snow.

SQUARE PROFILE DIVE
A type of dive that involves staying at one particular depth for the entire dive and then ascending directly to the surface.

SQUEEZE
A pressure-related injury resulting from failure to equalize on descent. Air-filled cavities such as the sinuses, middle ear, and mask are most commonly affected.

STANDING CURRENTS
Currents that are steady and consistent.

STORM
Atmospheric disturbance characterized by winds from 56 to 65 knots per hour.

SURFACE AIR CONSUMPTION RATE (SAC RATE)
The rate of underwater air consumption converted to an equivalent surface rate; commonly measured in psi/minute. See Chapter 4 for information on calculations.

SURFACE CHOP
Short, small waves resulting by wind disturbing the water's surface.

SURFACE INTERVAL TIME (SIT)
The time spent on the surface between dives; must be at least 10 minutes, but a minimum of one hour is suggested.

SURGE
The foreward and backward motion of waves as they recoil against the bottom.

SWELL
Smooth, consistent waves which become surf as they approach the shoreline.

SWIMMING ASCENT
See EMERGENCY SWIMMING ASCENT

T

TACHYCARDIA
Excessive rapidity of the heart beat.

TAG LINE
See LIFE LINE

THERMOCLINE
A subsurface layer of water characterized by rapid temperature and density changes with depth.

TIDAL CURRENTS
Currents that are influenced by changes in the tide.

TIDAL VOLUME
The quantity of air that is inhaled and exhaled with each breath.

TIDE
A long period wave which is noticeable as the periodic rise and fall of the ocean surface along coastlines. Tides are caused by the gravitational pull of the sun and moon.

TRAIL LINE
See LIFE LINE

TRANSITORY CURRENTS
Unpredictable currents

TROUGH
The lower portion of a wave between its CREST and the surface of the ocean.

TYMPANIC MEMBRANE
A thin membranous partition separating the external ear from the middle ear.

TYPHOON
A high velocity storm of 150 to 300 miles in diameter.

U

UHMS
Undersea and Hyperbaric Medical Society

UNDERTOW
Currents running toward the sea found near the bottom of a sloping beach that results from the return of water carried to the shore by wave action.

UPWELLING
A process which carries nutrient-rich subsurface water upward to the PHOTIC ZONE.

V

VERTIGO
A loss of the sense of balance accompanied by dizziness and confusion.

W

WAVE HEIGHT
The distance from the lowest portion of a wave (TROUGH) to the highest potion (CREST).

WHOLE GALE
A wind of 48 to 55 knots.

WINDWARD
The direction from which the wind blows; opposite of leeward.

Z

ZOOPLANKTON
Animal members of the plankton.

Reference Materials

The following compilation of books, periodicals, newsletters, and organizations is provided as a source of reference that will hopefully prove to be a valuable addition to this text. The information is presented in alphabetical order as per the individual headings. All books, periodicals, and newsletters were selected for their relevance, in one way or another, to the material covered in the preceding six chapters. From marine life to diving medicine, I have attempted to cover several subject areas that would be useful to solo divers (or for that matter, any divers) and would provide one with a good cross-section of diving-related information. The organizations listed were chosen for their overall importance to sport divers and because of the unique information that each provides.

BOOKS

A Medical Guide to Hazardous Marine Life
Auerbach, P.S.   (1987)
Progressive Printing Co.
Jacksonville, Florida

Advanced Diving: Technology and Techniques
National Association of Underwater Instructors
Montclair, California

Between Pacific Tides, Fifth Edition
Ricketts, Calvin, Hedgpeth, Phillips   (1985)
Stanford University Press
Stanford, California

Biology of Marine Life, Fourth Edition
Sumich, James L.   (1988)
Wm. C. Brown Publishers
Dubuque, Iowa

California Marine Life
Snyderman, Marty   (1988)
Marcor Publishing
Port Hueneme, California

Cold Weather and Under Ice Scuba Diving
NAUI/NDA Technical Publication Number 4
Somers, Lee H., Ph.D. (1973)
National Association of Underwater Instructors
Montclair, California

DAN Underwater Diving Accident Manual
Divers Alert Network (1985)
Duke University Medical Center
Durham, North Carolina

Dive Computers: A Consumer's Guide to History, Theory and Performance
Loyst, Huggins, Steidley (1991)
Watersport Publishing, Inc.
San Diego, California

Dive Rescue Specialist Training Manual
Linton, Rust, Gilliam (1986)
Dive Rescue, Inc./International
Fort Collins, Colorado

Diver's Almanac
Editor Bill Holdeman
Sports Almanacs, Inc.
Medford, Oregon

Diving Free
Eyles, Carlos (1978)
Watersport Publishing, Inc.
San Diego, California

Diving Medicine, Second Edition
Bove & Davis (1990)
Grove and Stratton, Inc.
New York, New York

Diving and Subaquatic Medicine
Edmonds, Lowery, Pennegather (1983)
Best Publishing Co.
Carson, California

Last of the Blue Water Hunters
Eyles, Carlos (1985)
Watersport Publishing, Inc.
San Diego, California

Marine Biology: Environment, Diversity, and Ecology
Lerman, Matthew (1986)
The Benjamin/Cummings Publishing Company, Inc.
Menlo Park, California

NOAA Diving Manual: Diving for Science and Technology, Second Edition
Edited by Miller, James W.
U.S. Government Printing Office
Washington, D.C.

Physiology in Depth: The Proceedings of the Seminar
Edited by Graver, Dennis (1982)
Professional Association of Diving Instructors
Santa Ana, California

Safety in Diving
Dueker, C.W. (1985)
Madison Publishing Associates
Menlo Park, California

Scuba Equipment: Care and Maintenance
Farley and Royer (1984)
Marcor Publishing
Port Hueneme, California

Scuba Life Saving
Pierce, Albert (1985)
Leisure Press
Champaign, Illinois

Search and Recovery
Erickson, Ralph D. (1983)
Professional Association of Diving Instructors
Santa Ana, California

The Amber Forest: Beauty and Biology of California's Submarine Forests
McPeak, Glantz, Shaw (1988)
Watersport Publishing, Inc.
San Diego, California

The Audubon Society Field Guide to North American Seashore Creatures
Meinkoth, Norman A. (1981)
Chanticleer Press, Inc.
New York, New York

The California Nutrition Book
Saltman, Gurin, Mothner (1987)
Little, Brown and Company
Boston, Massachusetts

The DAN Emergency Handbook
Lippman and Buggs (1989)
J.L. Publications
Victoria, Australia

The Encyclopedia of Recreational Diving
Professional Association of Diving Instructors
1251 East Dyer Road #100
Santa Ana, California 92705

The Physiology and Medicine of Diving, Third Edition
Bennett and Elliott (1982)
Best Publishing Co.
San Pedro, California

The Underwater Investigator
Teather, R. G. (Corporal, RCMP) (1983)
Concept Systems, Inc.
Fort Collins, Colorado

U.S. Navy Diving Manual
NAVSEA (1980)
Best Publishing Co.
Carson, California

Weather at Sea
Houghton and Sanders (1986)
International Publishing Company,
Highmark Publishing Ltd.
Camden, Maine

Women Underwater
Sleeper, Bangasser (1979)
DeepStar Publishing
Crestline, California

PERIODICALS AND NEWSLETTERS

Alert Diver: The Newsletter of the Divers Alert Network
Divers Alert Network
Box 3823, Duke University Medical Center
Durham, North Carolina 27710

AquaCorps: The Journal for Experienced Divers
AquaCorps
P.O. Box 1497
Aptos, California 95001

Discover Diving: The Diver's Journal
Watersport Publishing, Inc.
P.O. Box 83727
San Diego, California 92138

Diver Magazine
Seagraphic Publications Ltd.
10991 Shellbridge Way
Richmond, British Columbia,
Canada V6X 3C6

Fisher World Treasure News
Fisher Research Laboratory
Department NL-44
200 W. Willmott Road
Los Banos, California 93635

Ocean Realm
RAKU, Inc.
342 West Sunset Road
San Antonio, Texas 78209

Pressure: The Newsletter of the Undersea and Hyperbaric Medical Society
UHMS Diving Committee
9650 Rockville Pike
Bethesda, Maryland 20814

Scuba Times
GBP, Inc.
14110 Perdido Key Drive, Suite 16
Pensacola, Florida 32507

Sea Frontiers
The International Oceanographic Foundation
4600 Rickenbacker Causeway
P.O. Box 499900
Miami, Florida 33149-9900

Sources: The Journal of Underwater Education
NAUI Diving Association
P.O. Box 14650
Montclair, California 91763-1150

The Slate: Newsletter of the American Academy of Underwater Sciences
AAUS
947 Newhall Street
Costa Mesa, California 92627

Underwater USA
Press-Enterprise, Inc.
3185 Lackawanna Ave.
Bloomsburg, Pennsylvania 17815

Woman Diver
Suite 820 ST, 6631 Wakefield Drive
Alexandria, Virginia 22307

DIVING-RELATED ORGANIZATIONS

American Academy of Underwater Sciences (AAUS)
947 Newhall Street
Costa Mesa, California 92627

C.U.R.E. International
Center for Underwater Research and Exploration, Inc.
750 Knoll Street
Lindenhurst, New York 11757

Divers Alert Network (DAN)
Box 3823
Duke University Medical Center
Durham, North Carolina 27710

Hyperbarics International, Inc.
490 Caribbean Drive
Key Largo, Florida 33037
(Provides advanced training programs for Nitrox diving.)

National Association for Cave Diving (NACD)
P.O. Box 14492
Gainesville, Florida 32604

National Speleological Society-Cave Diving Section (NSS-CDS)
P.O. Box 950
Branford, Florida 32008

Professional Scuba Association, Inc.
2219 East Colonial Driive
Orlando, Florida 32803
(Provides advanced deep diving instruction and training.)

Index

A

B

C

D

E

F

fitness   28, 36, 37, 38, 40
free diving   39, 47, 48

G

gravity   56

H

heat exhaustion   42, 58
heat stroke   58
high-elevation diving   25
hyperbaric medicine   59
hypercapnia   55
hyperventilation   55
hypothermia   57
hypoxia   55

I

ice diving   24, 64
independent doubles   74, 75
independent scuba cylinders   77
independent systems   75

K

kelp   23, 24, 37, 66

L

lung overexpansion injury   63, 71

M

Mal de mer   32, 33
marine biology   18
maximum dive time   59
maximum pulse rate   40
medicine   18

mental fitness   34
mental preparedness   36
military diving   20
mixed gas   51

N

neutral buoyancy   56
nitrogen narcosis   39, 42
Nitrox   51
no-decompression limits   59, 60

O

obesity   41, 42
oceanography   18
Octo +   68, 69
octopus/safe-second   62, 64, 65, 69, 73, 74
ostrich syndrome   46
out-of-air   11, 48, 62, 64, 73
out-of-air emergency   62, 65, 66, 71, 77
outgassing   42, 59
overeating   42
overhead environments   63
oxygen deficiency   55

P

photography   12, 21
physical conditioning   21, 36, 48
physical fitness   34, 36, 40, 47, 54
physiology   18, 40
pony bottle   74, 75
primary air supply   66
primary second-stage   65
proficiency   32
proper breathing pattern   55
psychological fitness   40
pulmonary fitness   42

R

recreational diving   10, 11, 13, 64
redundancy   51, 53, 64, 65, 72, 75, 77
reefs   24
reserve regulator   74

Notes

Notes